Prophecy and Power

ADONIS
HOURIA ABDELOUAHED

Prophecy and Power

Violence and Islam II

Translated by Julie Rose

polity

Polity Press
65 Bridge Street
Cambridge CB2 1UR, UK

Polity Press
101 Station Landing
Suite 300
Medford, MA 02155, USA

ISBN-13: 978-1-5095-4214-7
ISBN-13: 978-1-5095-4215-4 (paperback)

A catalogue record for this book is available from the British Library.

Library of Congress Cataloging-in-Publication Data
Names: Adūnīs, 1930- interviewee. | Abdelouahed, Houriya, interviewer. | Rose, Julie, 1952- translator.
Title: Prophecy and power : Violence and Islam II / Adonis, Houria Abdelouahed ; translated by Julie Rose.
Other titles: Prophétie et pouvoir. English
Description: English edition. | Cambridge, UK ; Medford, MA, USA : Polity Press, [2021] | "Originally published in French as Prophétie et pouvoir. Violence et Islame II (c) Editions du Seuil, 2019." | Includes bibliographical references. | Summary: "A penetrating analysis of Islamic power by the greatest living Arab poet"-- Provided by publisher.
Identifiers: LCCN 2020048685 (print) | LCCN 2020048686 (ebook) | ISBN 9781509542147 | ISBN 9781509542154 (paperback) | ISBN 9781509542161 (epub)
Subjects: LCSH: Violence--Religious aspects--Islam. | Violence in the Qur'an. | Islam and politics--21st century. | Islam and state--21st century. | Adūnīs, 1930---Interviews.
Classification: LCC BP190.5.V56 A355213 2021 (print) | LCC BP190.5.V56 (ebook) | DDC 297.2/7--dc23
LC record available at https://lccn.loc.gov/2020048685
LC ebook record available at https://lccn.loc.gov/2020048686

Typeset in 11 on 13pt Minion Pro
by Fakenham Prepress Solutions, Fakenham, Norfolk NR21 8NL
Printed and bound in Great Britain by Short Run Press

For further information on Polity, visit our website:
politybooks.com

What he wanted was power; in Paul, the priest once more reached out for power; he had use for only such concepts, teachings and symbols as served the purpose of tyrannizing over the masses and organizing mobs. What was the only part of Christianity that Mohammed borrowed later on? Paul's invention, his device for establishing priestly tyranny and organizing the mob: the belief in the immortality of the soul – that is to say, the doctrine of 'judgement'.

Nietzsche, *The Antichrist*

Contents

1

God, 'The Messenger of Muhammad'?

H: In *Violence and Islam*, we tried to explain the failure of the Arab Spring.[1] We will pursue our thoughts here about an uprising that occurred at the same time as the rise of Islamic State (IS, also known as ISIS and Daesh), whose flag proclaims for all the world to see this testimonial of faith: *Allāh rasūlu Muhammad* (God is the Messenger of Muhammad). That symptomatic inscription reveals a historic truth we'll try to unpack. How did God become the Messenger of Muhammad? Which is another way of saying: what exactly is Islamic State the name of?

A: It would be prudent to say first off that we're not criticizing for the sake of criticizing, and that we refuse to adopt Arab and/or Western political and ideological stances. Our work is an attempt to establish an objective understanding of Islam, from a practical and theoretical point of view, in order to make a distinction between those who read the religious corpus, in particular the Qur'an, with their own interests in mind, and those who read it to get closer to God. We'll begin by summarizing the principles of Qur'anic exegesis and the way the Qur'an and the *ḥadīth*[2] were constituted, so that our readers can understand the status of the prophet in Islam and the connection Muslims have maintained with the person of Muhammad for fifteen centuries. So we'll be tackling the task of considering Muhammad the man as absolute (ultimate, supreme) authority. This is how we understand the phrase used by IS, 'God is the Messenger of Muhammad', which means 'God wants what Muhammad wants'.

H: The issue of reference is closely connected to the writing of history whereby no distinction was made between historic facts and legends. So we'll be contributing to the deconstruction of a corpus that has governed us from the moment it was first founded by transforming 'legend history', to use Michel de Certeau's expression, into 'work history'.

A: As for the title, *Violence and Islam*, let's just say that the issue of violence is intrinsically bound up with Islam as an institution: first, Muhammad proclaims that there is no hierarchy between the prophets,[3] but at the same time he claims he's the Seal of the Prophets. Second, proclaiming himself the Seal of the Prophets, he, unlike his predecessors, is the bearer of ultimate truths. Third, and this is the consequence of what I've just recalled to mind, Islam, instead of being universal, finds itself split or riven into believers (the faithful) and non-believers (infidels), and, more precisely, into Muslims and non-Muslims.

H: The Seal of the Prophets doesn't adhere to any kind of continuity, but is all about revisions and excisions. While acknowledging the prophets who preceded him, Muhammad strips other religions of their singularity, if not of their essence, thereby destroying the basis on which those religions rest.

A: Absolutely. And we should examine what the end of prophecy means. Does it stem from a divine decision? And how can we be sure God said those last words to his last prophet? What sense are we to make of a Revelation that was meant to be the closure of prophecy?

H: What sense, indeed, are we to make of a prophecy that announces its own end? We grew up with phrases no one ever questioned. The moment they touched on the prophet of Islam, we internalized them as absolute truths. We never, for instance, looked into the verses that criticized the Jews, the first monotheists: 'twisting with their tongues and traducing religion',[4] or 'perverting words from their meanings'.[5] In relation to what truth is there twisting? And when it says of Jesus, 'they did not slay him, neither crucified him',[6] it's not just the basis of Christianity that is thereby attacked, but the event itself.

A: This points to the huge contradictions that are strewn throughout the Text and that merit a study that's not just theological but also anthropological and historical. We need to reconsider the relationship between Islam and the other religions of Arabia, to revisit and analyse the conflicts within Islam itself, and also to proceed to a linguistic analysis. That way, we might be able to see how God became a Muslim property. The logic that dominates the Text and the corpus of the *sunna*[7] is this: if God exists, he can only be Muslim. Doesn't the verse say precisely, 'The true religion with God is Islam'?[8]

H: Is that any different from Judaism, which chooses itself a people?

A: It's very different from Judaism, as the God of Islam has nothing more to say since he's said his last word to his last prophet, who, towards the end of his life, states: 'Today, I have perfected my good deeds and chosen [*raḍītu*],[9] for you, Islam as religion.' And: 'You are the best nation ever brought forth to men.'[10] God thereby becomes part of Islam and not the other way round. This internal contradiction puts Islam in a bind. Because saying that God is a Muslim makes God, and consequently the truth, a possession of Muhammad's. Where was God for fifteen centuries? How come he didn't show himself earlier, given that man has been on Earth for millions of years?

H: Adonis! There's historical time and there's mythical time. Religion is tied up with the second. And one could retort that God had sent other prophets, well before Islam.

A: It's good to raise the question because it allows us to clear up a very important point: the verses refer to the Jews, not because of their doctrine, but because they fought Muhammad.

H: In Ṭabarī's commentary, we read that the Jews perverted their Holy Book,[11] but he doesn't say what the *taḥrīf* (the perversion of meaning) consists of, or in relation to what. Apart from that, we find ourselves confronting an extremely problematic and very violent act of appropriation in terms of theory because Abraham, the Jewish patriarch, becomes a Muslim.[12] The Jewish prophets are given as Muslim and this, even before the advent of Islam.

A: You're right to talk about violence because Islam, in theory, adopted what came before it but cancelled it out, in practice, at the same time. The religions all became Muslim. Just read the verse we mentioned above: 'The true religion with God is Islam.'[13] As I said a moment ago, God himself became a Muslim. And the world was thus turned into a property of Islam. That goes against the truth, against humankind and against God himself. It's the height of violence.

H: Yet while cancelling out all that came before it, the Qur'an makes use of Babylonian and Sumerian myths and legends, such as the Flood, which is in the *Epic of Gilgamesh*. It also took up narratives from the Bible, such as the story of Job, the story of Noah, of Moses …

A: Unlike Christianity, which can be considered a revolution, since it transformed the very idea of God, Judaism doesn't contain anything new, except the idea of the chosen people. Islam is like Judaism, and the *shar'* (Muslim law)[14] is a bit too much like Jewish law for comfort. There are differences in the details, but the core remains the same. Yet Judaism evolved compared to Islam for it became part of Western civilization. We find Jewish intellectuals who don't believe in the Bible and don't concede that it's sacred in any way. This liberty is not available to Muslims. You could even say that the Jewish spirit is more alive and well in the Muslim religion than it is in the Bible. But we need to go further: unlike Jews or Christians, who have the right to change religion, Muslims don't have the right to change religion. Assassination awaits anyone who is tempted to leave Islam. He is counted among the apostates, and his murder, consequently, becomes lawful.

H: I'd just like to make it clear that, when you say 'Assassination awaits anyone who is tempted to leave Islam', you're actually talking about someone born into a Muslim family or a Muslim environment, or on Muslim soil. Since there is no baptism, the child is born a Muslim, even if the parents are atheists or communists. And he or she is not free to change faith later on in life. From the moment Islam becomes a 'genetic' inheritance, there is no freedom.

A: I've often talked about this issue, as you know. I see Islam as a political and economic *coup d'état* – just like

Judaism, in fact. Islam needs to go through an internal revolution.

H: Any such revolution comes up against a corpus that produced the figure of a prophet as an absolute authority. And this human corpus itself became an absolute authority. Our task consists in reminding people of this and analysing it.

A: How come the heaven of prophecy closes forever after? And how come the *ḥadīth* becomes the absolute authority? We might even say that you can criticize God but not Muhammad. Criticizing Muhammad boils down to cancelling out the authority. That's one reason why the words used to describe Muhammad's greatness reveal themselves to be a political construct. This latter – which has been promoted to the same rank as the divine Text – becomes the essential origin of the *shar*ʿ, and so the *sunna*[15] can then be imposed as the essential principle of jurisdiction and thought.

H: Yet when we manage to get out from under this ban on thinking and we read the corpus with a critical eye, we very quickly see it's a text that's human, all too human. The jurisprudence that has governed us to the present day, and which draws largely on the *sunna*, arose as a way of legitimizing practices that saw the light of day when the religion was founded.

A: But what is the *sunna*? What is this corpus that was to create such discord between Muslims? Conflicts over the *sunna* have sparked a political war within Islam. There were a great number of dissident groups in the beginning, when it was founded: seventy, more or less, such as *Al-Ḥarūriyya*, *Al-Qadariyya*, *Al-Jahmiyya*, *Al-Murjiʾa*, *Al-Rāfiḍa*, *Al-Jabriyya*, *Al-Khawārij*, *Al-Shīʿa*,

Al-Bāṭiniyya ... All these groups were exterminated. No other religion has had so many divisions that were literally spread and dominated by the *jamāʿa*.[16] When *Shāfiʿī*[17] says: 'He who gives his view on the subject of the Qur'an is in error, even if what he says is true', he says this in the name of the *jamāʿa*. This rules out the notion that an individual can choose for himself, based on his experience or the extent of his knowledge, for example. Interpretation henceforth requires some kind of a political power. In the eyes of the *jamāʿa*, the individual has no existence as a free autonomous being in control of himself and of his thoughts.

H: There have also been divisions and schisms within Christianity.

A: Not with the same degree of violence. In Islam, such divisions are over the divine essence.

H: In Christianity, too. Much was written about the issue of the divine essence by the Church Fathers. Tertullian, among others.

A: In Islam, political power has always triumphed. From the moment Islam was founded, civil society has always been under the domination of the political power. So, when people talk, today, about change, it's not so much about changing the social or political structure as about a succession of individuals exercising power.

H: In Christianity, you also had the despotism of the Church. Only, the West has seen secularization, whereas *we* come up against something unthought-of, something that cannot let itself be thought, by virtue of the fact that everything that touches either closely or remotely on prophecy is regarded as sacred.

A: In Islam, there is no thinking outside religion. When the verses incite us to reflect, what you have to understand by this is that we need to reflect based on what the Qur'an says. Just as there is no truth outside the Qur'an, so there is no thought outside the Text. Thinking comes down to thinking through the Text based on the Text and not based on the world.

H: Ignorance plays an undeniable role in the maintenance of this lockdown on the Text, and even its idealization. Many Muslims don't know that the word *ḥanīf*,[18] which refers to their religion, is an epithet that predated Islam and was only applied to Islam by Muhammad much later on. The *ḥanīfiyya* religion was preached by Maslama – who was actually known as Maslama al-Ḥanafī – in southern Arabia, namely Yemen, which is under bombardment today.

A: Indeed, as a religion *ḥanīfiyya* was spread widely throughout South Arabia.

H: In today's Muslim imagination, Muhammad was born a Muslim. Since there's a ban on thinking, people don't even ask themselves what a Muslim could possibly have been before Islam came along. Well, the hagiographical texts claim he was *wathanī* (a pagan). In his excellent book, Muhammad Mahmūd[19] cites Al-Kalbī as saying that Muhammad, like the people of his tribe, was an idolater. We read: 'For the Quraysh,[20] Al-'Uzzā was the greatest god. It has come down to us that the Messenger of God one day said that he'd made an offering to Al-'Uzzā.'[21] Certain *ḥadīths* cited in Ṣaḥīḥ al-Bukhārī[22] fit in with that.[23]

A: Of course. Muhammad was born into a pagan context. But do the works make reference to his religious practices from the time before Islam?

H: *Laqad 'ahdaytu li-l'uzzā shātan wa 'anā 'alā dīni qawmī* (I made an offering to Al-'Uzzā when I practised the faith of my community). That's a *ḥadīth* cited by Al-Kalbī and by Al-Bukhārī. The latter goes further, stipulating that Muhammad was a *wathanī*, whereas other people in Mecca were *ḥanafiyyūn*. He converted later to *ḥanīfiyya*.

A: The fact that he was a pagan and that he converted to Islam might encourage Muslims to see this as a positive point: God chose him.

H: Al-Jāḥiẓ[24] reports what Muhammad said to Zayd ibn 'Amrū bin Nufayl: *Yā Zayd! Innaka fāraqta dīna qawmika wa shatamta ālihatahum* (O, Zayd! You have cut your ties with the religion of your community and you have insulted their divinities). There are two things we might say about that. First, Muhammad defended paganism as a faith and practice in Quraysh. Second, people in his tribe went on to renounce paganism.

A: Muhammad converted to *ḥanīfiyya* under the influence of Waraqa ibn Nawfal, his wife Khadīja's cousin, who was a man of immense erudition, a man who knew all about the religions and religious practices of Arabia.

H: The Qur'anic verse fits in with Muhammad's conversion:

Did we not expand thy breast for thee,
and lift from thee thy burden,
the burden that weighed down thy back?[25]

The commentator Al-Ḍaḥḥāk[26] says that *wizr* (burden) is the associationism Muhammad lived surrounded by. Ṭabarī, for his part, explains that God expanded Muhammad's breast, opening his heart to the right path.

A: Muslims can interpret this story as proof of their prophet's greatness and of his victory over associationism. He is thereby an example to follow. The verse invites people to follow Muhammad's lead and abandon their old beliefs. The verse is to be applied to the whole of humanity.

H: Qutada[27] interprets 'burden' as 'Muhammad's grave sins which God has erased'.[28] We have a verse that says *wa wajadaka ḍāllan fa hadā* ('Did he not find thee erring and guide thee?').[29] It's clear that the change was gradual: Muhammad broke with idolatry, then adopted *ḥanīfiyya* before finally settling on Islam.

A: Mecca was a meeting place. Muhammad was well up on the customs of the peoples who flocked to Mecca for trade, bringing with them their stories, their beliefs and their religious practices. On top of that, he himself was involved in trade, which necessitated trips to Shām, today's Syria. This allowed him to get abreast of the civilizational and religious practices of the region.

H: The hagiographers don't specify the precise moment at which Muhammad dropped paganism for *al-Ḥanīfiyya*. We read that the Revelation began when he was forty years old, an age that was seen generally and traditionally as the age of reason. On the other hand, we don't have any precise historical details about his conversion to *ḥanīfiyya*.

A: All the hagiographies talk about the relationship Muhammad kept up with Waraqa ibn Nawfal. We know that the *ḥanīfiyyūn* were against paganism and respected Christianity and Judaism.

H: The *al-Ḥanīfiyya* religion really left its mark on Islam. The pilgrimage existed in *al-Ḥanīfiyya*, just as prayer did, just as fasting did. Islam would later be defined as the *ḥanīfa* (pure or original) religion. The Qur'an mentions *ḥanīfan* ten times, seven times linking the expression to the religion of Abraham. The prophet of Islam was to adopt the term *ḥanīf* to refer to pure Islam.[30]

A: We might remember the figure of Maslama. His education was very similar to that of Muhammad's and he was known as Maslama al-Ḥanafī. The name was changed to Musaylima al-Kadhdhāb, the forger (liar, falsifier).

H: He preached the *dīn ḥanīf*, the pure religion – the Islam that was to take on the adjective *ḥanīf*, that was to fight Maslama. Ma'rūf al-Ruṣāfī[31] says: 'If Maslama had not been defeated, Islam would have had a different face.'

A: This is where it would be interesting to reread the history of Islam and explore the religious and anthropological context of Arabia in its relationship with other countries. Mecca was a great scene of religious and commercial rivalries.

H: Zayd ibn 'Amrū bin Nufayl, who was a *ḥanīf*, played a major role in Muhammad's religious awakening. Zayd refused to make offerings to the divinities of Quraysh. Muhammad, we read, was later to grant him a place in paradise. That's how he expressed his gratitude to Zayd.

A: These are interesting examples that invite us to look more closely at the way Muhammad's religious awakening evolved through contact with influential people in Arabia. But we need to go further and question the very notion of 'prophecy'. What is prophecy? How did Muhammad succeed in creating a Muslim climate? How was he able to create Islam?

H: The theme of being chosen is traditional and perfectly familiar, and prophecy is a very old concept. It already existed among the Sumerians. Today, we no longer ask ourselves the reason for being chosen. Well, the first Arab hagiographers noted the following thing: 'The Jews have their prophets and the Christians have their prophet. In contrast, the Arabs have no prophet.' This remark stresses the psychological dimension, namely the narcissism of a people or tribe deprived of the prestige of being chosen in the context of an Arabia haunted by tribal wars.

A: Quite. Islam as Revelation and prophecy can only be explained in light of the social, intellectual and economic conflict of the day. The story of Abraha al-'Ashram makes sense here. We should add that at the time there was another crisis, namely the fall of Byzantium which left the world without a great power.

H: I seem to recall that there are several versions of the life of Abraha al-'Ashram. Ṭabarī writes that Abraha built a cathedral at Sanaa (in Yemen) that was meant to compete with the pilgrimage to the Ka'ba, and that he tried to destroy the latter some time around 570–571. But his army was wiped out by illness and by the miraculous *abābīl* birds, which dropped stones on the army.[32]

A: The conflict between Abraha and the Meccans wasn't religious, it was economic and political.

H: Abraha wanted to get control of Mecca because it was on a trade route between Yemen and Shām. What's interesting is that pagan Mecca resisted Christianity, which existed in the north and in the south of Arabia. How did Muhammad later manage to convert Mecca to Islam? Was it 'progress in the life of the mind', to borrow the phrase Freud used in describing monotheism? Was it a desire for a distant world or, as we've suggested, the desire to enjoy the privilege of prophecy?

A: This is connected to the commercial genius of the Quraysh, who managed to generate such power. I don't think it's got anything to do with a spiritual need. The history of Islam is devoid of a spiritual horizon. I've talked about this often: the mystics, philosophers and poets do not represent institutional Islam.

H: Can we say that there was, nevertheless, a need on the part of the Arabs for a God who transcended the visible world and broke with the divinities man had made up himself?

A: I'd say that the Arabs had a great need for a reference point that could gather them together.

H: Are you alluding to the chaotic state Arabia found itself in – I mean the never-ending conflicts between the Jewish tribes and the interminable wars between the two Arab tribes, the al-'Aws and al-Khazraj?[33] Gathering together, at that point, takes on a political significance.

A: There were indeed many tribal wars and conflicts. The economic strength of the Quraysh was decisive: the people of Quraysh knew how to put their economic genius to work to gain hegemony over the region. And prophecy was the means of consolidating that hegemony. So prophecy is a Qurayshite invention. The passage from paganism to Islam, as you said, was gradual. In the beginning, Mecca kept its paganism and various rites set up a bridge between the old world and the new religion. In this area of the world, where tribalism was powerful, Quraysh triumphed, in actual fact, not from a tribal point of view but in terms of religion.

H: That fits in with the image the hagiographies painted of Muhammad, after the event. Before the coming of Islam, we read, he didn't get involved in tribal allegiances and he did his utmost to reconcile the tribes whenever they were in conflict.

A: Muhammad managed to take the tribal conflict to another level. And this stance of his, according to which 'I say nothing, it's God who says everything', shows his genius. Because from the moment it's God that's doing the talking and expressing himself, Muhammad is no longer part of the conflict.

H: He also drew on the cultural context of Arabia. When he recounts how he heard stones telling him 'peace and salvation are on you, O Messenger of God!' or Buhaira stipulating that a cloud protected Muhammad whenever he was on his travels, this appeals to the magical thinking and animism that were so widespread in Arabia at the time.

A: Muhammad knew how to give to a legend a scope and value that were divine. That was his masterstroke. What the Babylonians, Mesopotamians, Greeks, Romans and other peoples saw as imaginary constructions became, for the Muslims, divine truth.

H: There are two different levels: what Muhammad said, and what the hagiographers wove together as narratives and which are constructions created after the event. The problem is that these constructions have never been analysed as such. By way of example, apart from the cloud protecting Muhammad, Buhaira was supposed to have seen the Seal of Prophecy. It's as if the Seal of Prophecy were material, tangible, palpable, visible. Which is a de-metaphorization of, and a limiting of, the faculty of representation and imagination. Only, since sacralization rules out all questioning, Muslims still give these legends full credence, thereby investing them with the status of celestial truth.

A. Exactly. There was a certain exploitation of the cultural context and intellectual conditions of the time. When Muhammad speaks of *jinns*,[34] or spirits, he reinforces a belief and gives it religious legitimacy, as you say. He talks about Gabriel in a way that's similar to the way he talks about spirits. This begs the question: why did Muhammad adopt Gabriel?

H: Gabriel appears in the Old Testament. In the Book of Daniel,[35] *Gabar* means 'force' and *El* means 'God'. The Arab name Jibril (Gabriel) is very close to Gabar since the two languages have the same Semitic roots. In the New Testament, Gabriel announces the birth of John the Baptist, and he is the angel of the Annunciation.[36] The angel is a familiar figure in monotheism. He is designated as the luminous face, while Satan is the dark face.

A: Why does Muhammad choose Gabriel?

H: Maybe because in the imaginary realm, traditionally and classically, divine dictates require an intermediary, and that intermediary is an angel. Islam did in fact draw on the traditions and teachings of the time. The story of Satan (the Devil) – such as it's related in the Gospel of St Matthew – who comes along and vainly tempts Jesus, was to be taken up by Muhammad on his own behalf.

A: But the Gospels don't constitute a revealed divine text.

H: Gabriel already existed as a Messenger of God. Muhammad takes Gabriel up again as a Messenger of Revelation, but Islamizes him by giving him other roles, such as being a warrior fighting alongside Muslims in battle. Gabriel took on the guise of a friend of Muhammad's or a defender, or counsellor … Which can't fail to remind us of Zeus's metamorphoses in the Greeks or Jupiter's in the Romans.

A: It's all very complex, since Muhammad, who is God's emissary, steps aside to make way for Gabriel. In the various hagiographical texts, as in the *sunna* and in the Qur'an, all he did was repeat the word of Gabriel. Even though it was Gabriel who revealed to him that he'd been chosen. We need go over everything again, starting from scratch.

H: Just as we need to go back over the story of Gabriel, who appeared to Muhammad, thereby plunging him into the throes of doubt (was he an angel or a devil?). The books of hagiography recount that the angel disappeared when Khadīja, Muhammad's wife, uncovered her hair. Head hair is the pubic hair of the mother, Freud tells us. From a psychoanalytical point of view, the story stacks up. On the other hand, from a historical point of view, this story proves to be a late construction, as the veil was only imposed on Muhammad's wives in Medina, and this was only after Khadīja's death.

A: Of course, it's a made-up story, which was only written very late in the day. To get back to Gabriel, Muhammad was able to create a pyramidal hierarchy: he obeys Gabriel who, himself, obeys God. What I'd like to do is deconstruct the structure of power in Islam. Why is power so important in the Arab world? Why does it take up the whole stage?

H: To work on the overlap of politics and religion, we need to go back over the texts that constitute the corpus of Islam. Let's start by way of example with the phrase: *bu'ithtu li-l-nāsi kāfatan* (I have been sent for the whole of humanity): if they do not believe in me, it is for the Arabs, if they do not believe in me, it is for Quraysh, if they do not believe in me, it is for *Banū Hāshim*,[37] if they do not believe in me, it is for myself.[38] What sense could a prophecy that can do without other people possibly have?

A: The 'if' is very important. To my mind, prophecy is the operation of power, and so, it's political. Muhammad is the one who drew up this political agenda. The Qur'an says: 'I have not created jinn and mankind except to serve Me.'[39] The aim of the creation of mankind is to serve God, to worship Him. Worship is absolute submission to God's will. How will God's will be translated? Muhammad was the first model of such submission. Hence the: 'I say nothing by myself. Everything comes to me from God. And I obey God.' He asks other people to submit to his word, just as he has submitted to Gabriel, who submitted to God. The *shar'* was invented so that this submission could be firmly rooted in people's minds and the social fabric. As a result, we can say that Muslims are born intellectually obedient and submissive. Islam, fundamentally, is not just a faith but a *shar'* that you have to apply and to which you have to submit.

H: I might seize this opportunity to say that people who translate 'Islam' by 'peace' are a bit too quick off the mark, reducing as they do all the complexity of the term.[40] If 'Islam' comes from *s.l.m*, which gives us *salām* (a general salutation, like 'hello') and *silm* (peace), that sense of the word is qualified by a reservation, the author of *Lisān al-'Arab* tells us, since the greeting (a kind of blessing) is only meant for those who have taken the path of *al-hudā* (the 'right path'), preached by the Text. A *salīm* heart is a heart free of unbelief. Submitting to God is then understood as 'submitting only to the laws of the *sharī'a* (sharia)' set out by the prophet. Sharia becomes 'submitting before the conqueror'. And since the Arab language is full of *'aḍḍād* (words with opposite meanings), *salām* also refers to the individual who enjoys peace every bit as much as the person who surrenders before the conqueror, or before his own impulses, for *al-istislām* means *al-inqiyād* (submitting when faced with excessive conduct).

A: From a linguistic point of view, the word 'Islam' doesn't refer to peace, unless we think of acquiescence, submission, obedience as peace (*salām*). Moreover, Islam was not founded as peace. Quite the opposite: it saw the light of day as wars and conquests. It imposed a very particular 'peace' by forcing non-Muslims to convert. Finally, Islam is not only a faith, but the application of the *shar'* that governs the Muslim's political space as well as his social space, as I just said. And the vast majority of Muslims dutifully submit in their thinking and in their daily practice to this sharia. Alive or dead, Muhammad remains the guide for that majority.

H: Asking questions is a first step on the road to rescuing yourself from this voluntary submission. The texts tell this story: when Gabriel asked Muhammad to read, he replied, '*mā aqra'?*' (what can I read?). A different version says '*lastu bi-qāri*''(I can't read). It's this second version that's the most widespread. To reinforce the prophecy, they created the image of an illiterate prophet Gabriel dictated everything to.

A: I can't *not* express my amazement. How can you say, 'I was visited by an angel and he spoke to me'?

H: When the Qurayshites asked Muhammad why he was the only one ever to see the angel and why he didn't work miracles, Gabriel swiftly whispered this prompt in reply: 'Yet if they see a sign they turn away, and they say "A continuous sorcery!"'[41] And: 'Even so not a Messenger came to those before them but they said, "A sorcerer, or a man possessed!"'[42] And so, Muhammad's strength resides in this counter to the lack of proof. I agree with you when you raise the political aspect and the economic aspect. Yet, the psychological aspect is undeniably powerful.

A: That's for sure. We could say that the practice and experience of trade were extremely advantageous for

Muhammad. He knew how to cultivate the art of conversation and the faculty of persuasion. And so he managed to convince people that he was a representative of God on Earth, thus going from the status of trader or caravanner to that of Messenger of God. That remains an undeniable proof of his genius. I said a moment ago that Muhammad submitted to the angel who submitted to God and so on. In fact, the prophecy was a *taqwīl* of Allah's.[43] God spoke according to his prophet's desires. For a quarter of a century, God listened to what Muhammad wanted.

H: That's what little Aïsha summed up when she said: 'I feel that God rushes to satisfy your desires.' That's an extraordinary way of putting the power of Muhammad's desire, a desire that made even Heaven bend to it.

A: In fact, instead of talking about *nubuwwa* (prophecy), we need to coin a different term: *al-taqwīl*. That is, the act of making God say what man wants. Claiming that every word he uttered came to him from God, Muhammad became immortal. The Qur'an had the role of immortalizing him, and killing off all the other prophets in the process. We could even say that the first anti-Semite was the Semite God.

H: We should also add that the illiteracy they invented for Muhammad only reinforced the notion of divine inspiration. Can a trader be illiterate?

A: If Muhammad only said what was instilled in him by God, this also means he can never have read the other books.

H: The logical consequence that follows on from that construction is that, for Muslims, the great role model is a person who knows nothing. What a catastrophe!

A: Actually, this all stems from a determination to sacralize the person of Muhammad. And every caliph repeating the words of the prophet had a hand in his immortalization.

H: 'I am the truth that speaks.' I don't think we've really registered the importance of that idea, meaning the manufacture of a human who transcends humanity.

A: And yet, a Muslim must believe that God dictated everything to Muhammad. There is a big difference with Judaism there. Both the Old Testament and the New Testament acknowledged the biblical prophets. Islam, on the other hand, merged them into a single one. Muhammad becomes the sole and unique prophet in an Arabia that was crawling with them.

H: To sweep aside all the civilizations that came before the advent of Islam, along with all the prophets, diviners, poets … of Arabia, you'd have needed great strength and to be incredibly cultivated.

A: And yet, what was the reason Muhammad was so hesitant and troubled? Why did he think of suicide?

H: The hagiographers think the reason had to do with his visions. He was afraid of being a man possessed, a madman. That said, you're right to put the question again. The sacredness of the person of Muhammad prevents all reflection on Muhammad. We still haven't been able to do what Michelangelo did when he gave Moses two horns, or to tear apart the founder of Islam the way Freud did Moses, the man.

A: So, we mustn't be daunted by the question, even if there is no answer, for the moment. Muhammad was a trader and, logically, his education didn't encourage doubt. How did this grandiose and untouchable side come to see the light of day? What need did it fulfil?

H: He was made sacred. But in a symptomatic way his humanity came back into play on the narrative stage. We read: 'The prophet of God wanted to defecate and asked two palm trees to come closer so as to shelter him. Aïsha also wanted to go. But when she got to the palm trees, she said, "I can't see what you did, O Messenger of God!" And Muhammad replies, "The Earth swallows up the excreta of prophets."'

A: It's magic! Faeces turn to gold.

H: From a psychoanalytical point of view, the symbol of excrement is worth its weight in gold. But this tale of anality shows the other aspect of the collective imagination, which wavers between the grandiose figure and the human person. As if the ideality that makes the person of Muhammad untouchable was overtaken by the human aspect, but in an anal mode.

A: In *Lisān al-'Arab*, *siḥr* (magic) means 'the transformation of the reality of a thing into another', or 'to make believe something that is not'. You could say, then, that the world of *janna* (paradise) and of hell are magical.

H: Magical because they contradict the reality principle and the laws of logic and thought.

A: Except that the moment we're dealing with the word of God, the imaginary becomes reality. Even if it contradicts reality and reason, the word of God becomes absolute truth. A Muslim must therefore believe in the existence of the houris of paradise who go back to being virgins after each deflowering. In fact, Muslims live and die lured by two kinds of magic: the magic of this Earth, full of conquests and spoils, and the magic of a heaven that's packed with houris, ephebes, and rivers of milk and honey.

H: Everywhere, your urges are satisfied.

2

The *Ghazawāt*:[1] The Violence Involved in the Foundation of Islam

H: The foundation came about through the force of the sword, and the new religion spread in a climate of war, violence and terror.

A: Submission necessarily implies subjection, with the promise of paradise for those who die in combat.

H: We talk a lot about the violence of the Qurayshites in relation to Muhammad. Well, according to Sīrat ibn Hishām,[2] Muhammad was initially protected by his wife Khadīja, who was extremely powerful, and by his uncle Abū Ṭalib, who was a prominent Quraysh personage, and then, at a later stage, by tribal allegiance and association with the Qurayshites.

A: True, but there were assassination attempts on Muhammad.

H: Yes, the story goes that Muhammad was the target of a plot. But Gabriel, in a bid to foil the plot, asked Muhammad to sleep in his cousin ʿAlī's bed and ʿAlī to sleep in Muhammad's bed.

A: Gabriel got mixed up in everything. So, it's our duty to ask this question: how did it happen that a prophet could himself indulge in invasions and conquests? The first aim of a war or conquest is economic gain. Conquests can't have spirituality as an aim. Spirituality rejects violence.

H: There are numerous examples. We only have to look in Ṭabarī's *Tārikh* and in Al-Wāqidī – both dwell at length on the case of the Jewish tribe of Banū Qurayda. Ṭabarī tells how hundreds of individuals perished in a single day after being besieged. The number of beheadings was incredibly high. Those accounts are packed with details about the way the Muslims cut off the heads of so-called infidels and presented them to Muhammad, who himself also took part in the wars.

A: This is evidence and proof of the politico-economic aspect on which the foundation of Islam rests. The verses and the Revelation reinforced those practices by giving them a kind of legitimacy.

H: 'Muhammad', we read in Al-Wāqidī, 'congratulated Sa'd ibn Mu'ādh for having decapitated a lot of men, saying: "You applied the law of God that He may be sanctified". The next day, Muhammad gave the order to dig ditches in the marketplace and to bring in, one group after another, those Banū Qurayda who had been decapitated.' This violence became – in Muhammad's words – the law prescribed by God. Another passage tells how a *muhājir* (an emigrant from Mecca) asked Muhammad to pardon him, but the latter refused. Another passage says that Ibn Salūl intervened to save a number of people in the Banū Qurayda tribe who had fallen into captivity after the Battle of Badr. Muhammad at first refused to spare their lives. Next, faced with the prayers of Ibn Sall, who said to him, 'Do you want to eradicate seven hundred people in a single day?', Muhammad shot back: 'Let them live that they may be cursed, and may you be cursed too.'[3]

A: There are so many examples. The book of the *ghazawāt* is jampacked with details of unimaginable cruelty.

H: Muhammad, we read, '*bāʿa min al-dhurriyya*': he sold children. He sent some of the children north with 'Uthmān ibn 'Affān and 'Abdul-Raḥmān ibn 'Awf, and some to Shām with Saʿd ibn 'Ubāda. With the money he made, he bought weapons and horses.

A: Like IS today.

H: And all under the nose of Gabriel, who also took part in conquests. The story goes that the day Saʿd ibn 'Ubāda died, Gabriel, who was wearing a turban on his head, questioned Muhammad. 'O Muhammad, who is this man for whom the gates of paradise opened and the divine throne trembled?' And Al-Wāqidī's book insists on the spoils amassed in terms of flocks and herds, captive women and goods of all kinds. In fact, IS is making us relive these early days of the foundation.

A: 'Muslims arrived in Al-Katība where the last surviving Jews had fallen back. After fourteen days of siege, Kināna knew they had to surrender. He asked Muhammad for permission to leave with the children and their families, thus abandoning all their goods, even their clothes, to the Muslims. Muhammad assassinated him, took the goods and the captives, etc.' That's just one example among many.

H: Some Muslims say, '*Mā shabiʿnā ḥattā fataḥnā Khaybar*' (We didn't know satiety until after the conquest of Khaybar).

A: The monstrous, gory side of the conquests requires a lot of time to be narrated, detailed. We could sum up by saying that it was the economic angle that drove the Muslims. That angle was shored up by Gabriel, who guaranteed them paradise. We might remember that when he entered Mecca a victor, the Meccans – in order to stay alive – were forced to convert to the new religion. This testifies to a big difference with Christianity. Those who wanted to keep their faith had to leave, abandoning all their goods. That's what's known as a climate of terror.

H: The consequence was that even if people didn't convert through conviction, the children who came into the world were born and grew up on soil that had become Muslim, in a context in which, from that point on, Islam was the only prevailing religion. That's a very important fact in the making of Islam.

A: It does indeed provide a context in which power revealed its enormous capacity to build an empire. In fact, the empire began to take shape just after the conquest of Mecca.

H: When the Quraysh converts emigrated to Medina, the economic problem made itself cruelly felt. It was then that the issue of invasions and conquests became paramount. One of the Ansar men said: 'Our swords are dripping with the blood of Quraysh. And the colossal booty proved our triumph over our enemies.' And since wars are always extremely costly, Muhammad took and sold part of the booty to pay back his debts.

A: That's one of the things that could explain the expulsion of the Ansar.[4] They were expelled even though they'd welcomed and housed Muhammad and the first migrants from Mecca. In actual fact, everything's connected. The Ansars' expulsion from the political arena is only one aspect of their expulsion from other domains, which was specifically to do with the gains that followed every conquest and the divvying up of goods.

H: I remember one point: when Muhammad arrived in Yathrib (Medina), and the people from Mecca and Medina swore solidarity and fraternity to each other, a man from Medina said to a Meccan emigrant: 'I have two wives. Do you want one of them?' This was a made-up tale as the women from Medina were reputed to be strong, not submissive. But those who invented the story made so much of the fraternity between the two clans that they felt obliged to pin it on the women.

A: One reason why we need to deconstruct all this literature is that is so very demeaning, shameful and cruel. As far as history is concerned, the fifty years from the beginning of the foundation up to Saqīfa, and from Saqīfa up to Mu'āwiya,[5] were full of bloodshed.

H: The same cruelty runs through the works of Ibn Hishām, Al-Wāqidī, Ṭabarī and a whole host of others. In spite of this, the Arab and Muslim imagination has retained only the image of a generous prophet, crushed by hunger, poor and ascetic … whereas those works detail the divvying up of spoils between the members of Muhammad's family. We read, for instance, that 'the prophet gave each of his wives eighty *wasq*[6] of dates and eighty of wheat, to Ibn 'Abbās a hundred *wasq*, to 'Alī and Faṭima, three hundred *wasq*'.

A: Thanks to his successes on the battlefield and thanks to his political alliances, Muhammad became very rich and extremely powerful. As for the booty, it was distributed according to the ties of kinship in most cases, and according to the importance of a warrior's rank.

H: One of his companions said to him one day, 'You've become the richest man in Quraysh.' How is it that the collective memory has glossed over facts that abound in the works of reference?

A: That's the genius of Islamic power, specifically the creation of Islam as Revelation in order to gain politico-economic hegemony over the Arabian Peninsula. This begs the question: where does this power to persuade people that they're dealing with a divine message come from? Where does this force come from? It comes, it seems to me, from an ability to corrupt human beings. The events of what's known as the Arab Spring provide us with a crucial lesson here. That was a phenomenon that repeats aspects of what happened fifteen centuries ago.

H: IS, for instance, bears witness symptomatically to the violence of the foundation. It's what Freud called 'historical truth', and what we've been talking about today. It's a case of disinterring a historical truth camouflaged by a whole imaginary construct in which everything has been made sacred and so, has become unassailable.

A: The wars against Quraysh spread very rapidly and extended to other tribes. Muhammad was at once military chief, tactician, politician and prophet and this, from the Battle of Badr[7] to the end of his life. He's said to have taken part in twenty-seven battles.

H: Speaking of that battle, we read that it had its economic rationale. Abū Sufyān had heard that Muhammad was going to attack the Meccan caravaneers so as to take their goods. God helped the Muslims with a thousand angels. On the other hand, the Muslims lost the Battle of Uhud[8] – the hagiographers explain that the Muslims had disobeyed their prophet by throwing themselves on the spoils instead of waiting for the battle to end. If it hadn't been for that act of disobedience, God would have granted them five thousand angels, who would have helped them fight the unbelievers.

A: After the Battle of Badr, the Arabian Peninsula sank into an era of conflicts, battles, *saby* (the taking of captives, male and female) and violence such as it had never before seen. This fact is borne out in the works written by the Muslims who were the first hagiographers, people who can't be accused of unbelief.

H: Muhammad emerged from those wars and battles with many scars.

A: And enormous wealth.

H: We're looking at the violence that was part and parcel of the, not divine, but psychologically driven basis of the foundation.

A: It was all about force and nothing else. The sanctification of legends that predated the new religion reinforced the dogmatic aspect of Islam by drawing an aura around Muhammad that no prophet had ever had before him.

H: They say three people had written a pamphlet about Muhammad: two men, one of whom was an old man, and a woman. Ṭabarī says the woman was run through with a sword while she was breastfeeding her baby, the old man was also murdered, and the other man beheaded.

A: That's a well-known fact. Muhammad demanded that people bring him the heads of his enemies. Al-Wāqidī's book of conquests lists all these battles and their share of cruelty.

H: Ibn Mas'ūd, one of Muhammad's companions who became an authority in the passing on of the *ḥadīth*, says he had decapitated 'Abū Jahl and brought Muhammad his head. We read: 'I said: O Messenger of God, here is the head of God's enemy, 'Abū Jahl. Muhammad said: "There are no other gods but God." I threw the head in front of him. He praised God.'[9]

A: Facts to which were added legends like the involvement of Gabriel, who, as we've already mentioned, further sanctified the cruelty exercised against individuals and groups of people.

H: As for the involvement of heaven in the carnage, Al-Wāqidī tells how 'Abū Burda ibn Niyār said to Muhammad, after placing three heads on the ground in front of him: 'I killed two men. And I saw a tall man, all dressed in white, slice the head off a third man. I picked it up.'[10] The man all dressed in white was Gabriel. We also read about a Meccan man named Sa'd ibn al-Ashraf: 'The Muslims *kabbarū* (said: Allahu 'akbar)', and Muhammad realized they'd beheaded him. He said, '*aflaḥati al-wujūh*' (may faces be luminous). They replied '*wa wajhuka yā rasūla Allah*' (and may yours be blessed, O Messenger of God!). And they threw his head at Muhammad's feet and he thanked God for this victory.

A: That's an incredible story since the Messenger of God allowed people to lie to Sa'd in order to gain his trust only to murder him afterwards.

H: For a sum of money awarded to the plotters. His death is said to have greatly weakened the Jews.[11]

A: It's a way of saying Muhammad took part in the plots. Where was God when he was needed to rise up against the plots? How can Muslims continue to believe that all this came from God? Which would explain the lack of any reaction to the violence today. They haven't, to date, been able to criticize the violence. On the contrary, they've institutionally agreed to push for violence.

H: We also find descriptions relating not only to the Banū Qurayẓa, but also to other tribes such as Banū Khatama and Banū Naḍīr: 'They threw their heads in the wells of Banū Khatama.' Muhammad took a fifth of the spoils for himself and distributed the rest.

A: The wars increased their financial power. We know there were conflicts over the spoils, after the Battle of Badr. Muhammad is said to have been forced to intervene to distribute the spoils more equitably.

H: 'Did he not find you an orphan and he procured you a refuge? … He found you poor and he enriched you.'[12] The enrichment of Muhammad is recalled in a divine Text. Muhammad became so rich he promised his daughter Faṭima the Fadak, which was a tract of land. So, he not only had cattle, wheat and houses, but landed properties. He's even said to have had several oases.

A: That's the reason the government became the owner of what the prophet owned. The government stripped Faṭima of her inheritance by taking what was rightfully hers. Muhammad's wealth did not go to his daughter.

H: He was surrounded by strategists. Salmān al-Fārisī, considered the spiritual mystic of Islam, is the one who taught him the tactics of fighting in trenches (*khanādiq*, plural of *khandaq*).

A: We see the repercussions of these stories right up to the present day. The way they've destroyed Libya, Syria, Iraq, the Yemen … In fact, all this destruction springs from our tradition. Traditional Islam means trade and power. It means the violence that protects trade and power. And all of it is practised in the name of God.

H: If Islam made the death of its enemies licit, the death of believers posed a problem: 'How can God accept that people die when they're fighting for him?' Gabriel had this answer: 'Count not those who were slain in God's way as dead, but rather living with their Lord, and by Him provided.'[13] That verse cultivates the cult of the martyr.

A: 'God shall surely admit those who believe and do righteous deeds into gardens, underneath which rivers flow.'[14] Those who give themselves for their religion will have 'such fruits as they shall choose, and such flesh of fowl as they desire'.[15] As they lie, 'reclining upon couches lined with brocade, the fruits of the gardens nigh to gather'.[16] It was a series of acts of violence that stretched out over fifty years of the foundation. Muslims devoured each other. The founders were assassinated. Mu'āwiya reigned through violence. Al-Ḥasan, Muhammad's grandson, died poisoned. His brother Al-Ḥusayn was beheaded and others who supported them were annihilated.

H: That said, Al-Ḥasan and Al-Ḥusayn wanted to take power in the name of being descendants of the prophet. They didn't rise up against Mu'āwiya in the name of spirituality.

A: Religion, as we've said, was just a means of achieving power. But once the aura of the divine was bestowed entirely on Muhammad, he became the absolute authority on Earth. After that, no one had any further doubts about his person, or his words, or his actions. Everything he said and did was sacrosanct.

H: The picture painted by the hagiographers is far from idyllic. The violence wasn't directed exclusively at foreign tribes. In the heart of the new city of Medina, the Ansar and the migrants from Mecca fought over the spoils.

A: Of course. That's when the issue of conquests loomed too large. Love of gain fuelled rivalries.

H: The works also recount the fact that people who wished to have an audience with Muhammad to talk to him about the new laws established by the new religion had to pay for the audience. The question of *naskh*,[17] which we'll touch on later, has economic origins. The verse is clear:

> 'O believers, when you conspire with
> the Messenger, before your conspiring
> advance a freewill offering.'[18]

People complained because they didn't have the means to pay, *fa nusikhat al-āya* (the verse was abrogated). It lasted only an hour (*sāʿa min al-nahār*), say the commentators.

A: That's in keeping with the significance our countries and our culture give to a human being, to his relationship with another human being, with God and with the world. That story is extremely violent. And yet, as we keep saying, it remains sacred. And this sacralization today strongly compromises the emancipation of the individual, his life choices, his love life, his freedom, his subjectivity …

H: What's at issue is a static concept that constitutes identity for a lot of Arabs and Muslims. Identity becomes religious, without the individual Muslim giving himself the time to reflect on this unheard-of violence that runs through his history and constitutes the basis of a corpus that is his inheritance.

A: Islam was able to set up *tabaʿiyya*[19] as an ideology that put its stamp on Arab and Muslim culture. The sacralized power of Muhammad exceeds the limits of the human and transcends time and space.

H: To historicize his relationship with religion, the Muslim would need to put each verse in its context to rescue it from an absolute universality, and make it the result of a particular history.

3

Putting the Text to Work

H: The Qur'an puts itself forward as the Text. The events it mentions are drawn from the Old Testament. On top of that, when it announces an event, like the attack on the Ka'ba, it does so by mixing history with legend. Which makes any kind of historical intelligibility problematic.

A: In Islam, legends have become a fundamental part of history. Genies entered the daily lives of Muslims. From the moment the Qur'an mentions them, legends became realities.

H: It's a way of ensuring the prevalence of magical thinking …

A: … which then becomes a reality in daily life. That way, the world finds itself bound up with Islam and the world begins with Islam.

H: It does violence to thought when you no longer make a distinction between legend and historic fact.

A: Muhammad's conquests, his relations with women, the tribe, the spoils … all that, that's history. And whatever was external to history is brought into history – its own – by Islam. You're right, legend is jumbled up with historic fact. Even a legend like the one about paradise has become a truth. The individual dies for a houri who exists only in his imagination. Yet, that's become history.

H: This is the fabrication of a 'legend history' that has become history, since it's escaped the work of analysis, reflection and deconstruction. That's one reason Muslims just go on believing, right up to the present day, in the *abābīl* birds that defended the Ka'ba, as well as in the presence of Gabriel alongside the Muslim combatants. It's what comes out into the open in the *fatwās* we find on social media and have done since the emergence of IS.

A: The writing of history also poses an undeniable problem. For it's not human beings who write history but God, who loves human beings and angels. Islam overturned the world with this issue. It's an implausible story, the most grandiose ever written, and one that was fabricated by Muslims themselves. Angels and genies are bound up with the life and fate of Muhammad and of the Muslim.

H: When Muhammad was born, Ibn Hishām recounts, angels opened his chest to purify his heart for him. The verse, 'Did we not expand thy breast for thee?'[1] was taken in a literal sense even though *sharḥ*[2] can be understood not as a real, physical operation but in a metaphorical sense. Teaching and/or education can be part of the purification of the heart. Which undermines the status of representation in the works of people who've written commentaries on the Text and who have thereby taken part in the fabrication of a sacred story.

A: Not only are we supposed to believe it, but we don't have the right to doubt or contest or reason. And so we find ourselves faced with stories like that of *al-isrāʾ*[3] and *al-miʿrāj*[4] with no way of being able to question them. It says: 'Glory be to Him, who carried His servant by night from the Holy Mosque to the Further Mosque.'[5] And we're supposed to believe it. Out of duty!

H: The hagiographers report that the Meccans asked Muhammad to work a miracle. He then told them about his night trip. Faced with people who remained sceptical or who expressed their doubt, Gabriel revealed this verse:

> '... not a Messenger came to those before them
> but they said, "A sorcerer, or a man possessed!"'[6]

Even if you produce a whole raft of miracles, they won't believe. This point deserves some reflection because it's about the motive behind what's said. Here, what's said is its own pretext. In the Jewish imagination, Moses had a stick, and, in the Christian imagination, Jesus cared for lepers. You can, as André Miquel puts it, 'believe or dream'.

A: This means: you absolutely must believe without asking a single question. It's the very cancellation of thought.

H: We've reflected on what's known as 'the miracle' of the Qur'an. But by focusing on the style, we overlook the essential: the structure of the Text, namely the psychological process that cancels thought.

A: I'll put it another way. No prophet said: 'I am the last of the prophets.' Which comes down to implying: 'I incarnate the final knowledge.' The Muslim believes in that final knowledge. No other knowledge beyond the sayings of Muhammad. Thought comes up against this ultimate truth.

And believing works through repetition and subjection to the sayings of Muhammad. Basically, Islam is against knowledge because it is Knowledge, with a capital 'K'.

H: As if it were itself setting up an opposition between faith and knowledge.

A: Our prophet is Knowledge. There is no faith unless you believe that he is the ultimate Knowledge. This aspect of Islam ought to be studied, rethought, since it's an attack on the human. How can the divine word create slaves? God creates men free.

H: I'll seize this opportunity to remind us that slavery was not abolished or prohibited by Islam. Muhammad encouraged the freeing of slaves. But the hagiographers recount how he himself offered people slaves by way of thanks.

A: The tribute is essential in Islam. But let's say that if knowledge is the knowledge that flows from the Text, inviting people to reflect means all reflection has to be based on the Text and not on the world or any kind of thinking about the world. Under such conditions, is reflection still worthy of the name? If we want to reflect on issues involving the world and man, we ought to start with the Qur'an itself.

H: The Qur'an didn't get the scholarly work it merited. Studies tend to align with absolute respect for the literal without questioning the fundamentals from a linguistic, anthropological or epistemological point of view.

A: We might first remember that the Qur'an is a set of several versions. But the one adopted was the one chosen by 'Uthmān.[7]

H: Knowing that 'Uthmān burnt the other versions, and keeping only the one we have today. What was his choice based on? How did he make it? Why this one and not one of the others? Do we have the entirety of the Text or just part of it?

A: It was to avoid wars and scissions that Muslims accepted 'Uthmān's Qur'an. A way of turning the page. Whether the anthology cobbled together was true or false, Muslims today agree to accept the version they've got. It's no longer an academic issue. And the Text is the one that had the approval of all Muslims. It's not a question of looking for what was destroyed. The problem is that Muslims need to find the courage to deconstruct the Text as it is.

H: Only, to say that it's the arbitrary choice of 'Uthmān confers a human, all too human, status on the Text. What about the way it was written? How was the punctuation decided? According to what criteria? Was the meaning kept, but the expressions altered? Was it preserved just as it was revealed or dictated? What about the length of the suras? Whose memory were they based on? The majority of Muslims don't even know if the first verse is *Al-muddaththir* ('O thou shrouded in thy mantle', or Shrouded)[8] or *Al-'alaq* ('The blood clot').[9] So then, we'll unpack what we *can* unpack.

A: Even if we say that the Qur'an was completely derivative, taking everything from the other books, and particularly the Jewish books from which it got all its ideas, it remains the case that those ideas took another turn that distinguished it from Judaism and from Christianity and from the mythology that preceded them. The Qur'an is more caught up with life in the hereafter. God the One (*Al-Wāḥid*) and the Day of the Last Judgement take up virtually the whole stage.

H: It's our responsibility to point out the striking similarities with the Bible. At times, it's almost word for word.

A: We could say the same thing about the Bible and the legends that preceded it.

H: It's true that the Flood from *The Epic of Gilgamesh* was taken up in the Bible.

A: And the story of Job related in the Qur'an is taken from the Bible, which got it from a Sumerian poem. That said, the different themes that run through the Qur'an have acquired a different meaning because they're set in a different context. The Bible is linked to the life of a people and the culture of that people, and the same goes for the Qur'an.

H: This poses a political, ethical and intellectual problem: the Qur'an draws largely on the biblical text, but refers to Jews as undesirables,[10] idolaters,[11] accursed,[12] who incur the wrath of God[13] …

A: In actual fact, this rejection of the Jews dates from the Battle of Khandaq (the Battle of the Trench). Muhammad, in the beginning, saw the Jews as closely related believers.

H: Indeed, he mentions all the prophets that feature in the Bible: Moses, Joseph, Jacob, Job … Yet, he Islamizes them. Abraham features in the following manner: 'Abraham in truth was not a Jew, neither a Christian; but he was a Muslim and one of pure faith.'[14] Which reveals a major anachronism, for Islam would thereby precede Judaism and Christianity historically.

A: We could say the same thing about the Bible in relation to the Sumerian and Babylonian tradition.

H: But the biblical text doesn't say that Sumerian culture was Jewish.

A: You're right to insist on this point since, in Muslim doctrine, Islam *yajubbu mā qablah* cancels out whatever comes before it. But in general, and except for Christianity, the sacred texts proceed in the same manner. This is one reason why Christianity deserves to be seen as a real revolution, for it humanized God.

H: It's true that in the West we tend to speak of the Judaeo-Christian religion, whereas Christianity was a break with Judaism.

A: Which of course raises this question when we talk about religion: what's new in the world? And how do we introduce something new into the world? Borges talked about the death of the author. But what is an author? In fact, there is only one book, which man writes and rewrites over and over again, Borges said.

H: Only, does the book that gets rewritten cancel out the one that pre-existed it? Or is it written in continuity? This question of what is *ex nihilo* also questions the status of otherness and of History through the very fact of writing and rewriting.

A: Let's say, then, that the function of the Bible is very different from that of the Qur'an. The Bible remains linked to the history of the Jewish people and to the message addressed to the Jewish people.

H: If we take the example of St Paul, the most Jewish of the Christians, this is what he has to say: 'For we know that the law is spiritual: but I am carnal, sold under sin. For that which I do I allow not; but what I hate, I do.'[15] This emphasis on pulsional duality, on the tensions that inhabit and agitate 'the inner man', gives us pause for thought. What Paul says, which 'apparently' cancels out Judaism, is very different from what Muhammad or the exegetes say.

A: There are two different levels. First, there's the Text in itself. The Qur'an takes the Bible and, as well as various legends and myths, the *shar'*.[16] That's indisputable. But, and this is the second level, the function of the Qur'an and its context are completely different. If you compare the language of the Old Testament to the language of the Qur'an, the first is superior and shows great depth. The Qur'an took things, as I said, and gave them a different meaning. So we need to reflect, not on what it took, but on what it did with it. How did it fabricate this text? Remember that Muhammad was afraid and he hesitated to announce his prophecy.

H: All the more so as, at that time, Arabia was crawling with prophets, diviners and poets.

A: So then, we need to work on the Qur'anic Text itself. Islam took the law and the stories from the Bible and, from the Arabs, it took the language.

H: We've mentioned how the Arabs wanted to have a prophet. When the Qur'an says, 'Even so We have sent it down as an Arabic Qur'an',[17] that's a way of introducing prophecy into the middle of Arabia.

A: And the middle of Quraysh. He says 'Arabic' to signify that the Message was addressed to the geographical region.

H: With borrowings, as we said, from the Old Testament.

A: There are two periods of time: the first period is the Mecca period when Muhammad was close to the Jews, and then there's the Medina period, which bears witness to a major break with the Jews.

H: I think we need to reflect on the meaning of that closeness or rapprochement, and of the break. 'Never again did there arise in Israel a prophet like Moses', we read in Deuteronomy. It may be that Muhammad wanted to go further than Moses. Since the Bible says, 'never again did there arise in Israel a prophet like Moses', Muhammad declares himself the Seal of the Prophets. The consequence is that not only will no one ever again arise among the Arabs, but no one will ever again arise in the world. Which feeds into what you were saying about the Seal of Prophecy.

A: Not to mention that it's God speaking. We need to reflect on the historical conditions that allowed the advent of the Qur'an. Who wrote the Qur'an? Why did the Revelation take twenty-three years? These rather important questions remain sidelined, meaning neglected. So we need to study the facts from the inside.

H: We can't answer all those questions, but let's open up a working site, in Georges Bataille's sense of the term. We know that Waraqa ibn Nawfal, Khadīja's cousin, had a big influence on Muhammad, and it's said, on the quiet, that Waraqa and Buhaira contributed to the writing of the Qur'an.

A: That supports the sense of the hagiographers' texts on Muhammad's anguish and the way he hesitated to take on the role of prophet for twenty-odd years. Do we know why the Revelation was held up for three years?

H: We read in the hagiographies that Gabriel stopped his visits to Muhammad. His wife Khadīja told him that his Lord had abandoned him. Hence this verse that tells of the resumption of the Revelation: 'Thy Lord has neither forsaken thee nor hates thee.'[18]

A: Why did it take twenty-three years for the Revelation?

H: We can't answer that. But, luckily for intellectual enquiry, the question remains open.

A: To recap, moving on, what I've already put forward. Let's say first off that there is no novelty, either in Judaism or in Islam, when we compare them to the great figure of Zarathustra, for example. The sole novelty consists in the creation of a God who prefers his community to all others, and is thus a 'racist' God. Next, Christianity is characterized by the introduction of – or reconciliation with – a man-god. It was thus able to link up the pagan world and the monotheist world. Lastly, the Old Testament and the Qur'an recycled the old legends and stories by giving them the status of a Revelation emanating from God and therefore absolutely true. And the horrifying thing is that, in both books, the end justifies the means, namely recourse to vile and amoral behaviour like hypocrisy, trickery, betrayal, murder, looting and the sort of vengeance in the name of religion that goes hand in hand with a desire to expand.

H: That old-time desire to expand is making a comeback today and is being spread widely, via the Internet, by the Salafists who preach a return to sharia, and even the expansion of Islam in the world.

A: Violence is also to be found in the Old Testament. You can enter an enemy village and wipe out all the living, including the animals and poultry.

H: So is Muhammad the heir of Judaism?

A: Muhammad is a trader and a warlord, a politician and a prophet. But to answer your question, let's say the sole source of Islamic Revelation is Judaism. Islam is a sort of dialogue with Judaism. And the question of *nāsikh wa l-mansūkh*[19] precisely reveals the experimental side of the Qur'an.

H: The Qur'an in our possession is 'Uthmān's version, as we've said. Six other versions were burned. We read that Ibn Mas'ūd was beaten up because he refused to hand over his version to keep it from being destroyed. The question of how the Qur'an was written matters if only because it was committed to people's memories. Which of course raises the problem of reliability. When they say that the Qur'an was committed, in the beginning, to the memories of people who reproduced it absolutely unchanged, that's a way of denying the deficiencies in people's memories and how subjective human beings are. As if memory was infallible and human beings couldn't possibly make mistakes, or lie, or falsify the given material.

A: Obviously, we're dealing with a book written by human hands.

H: So we're back to the questions we started with. How was the Qur'an composed? To say it's a text that was constructed on the basis of a loss would fit a classic theme. But in the case of the Qur'an, it's said to have been written on whatever materials fate threw up: on leather, on paper or sometimes even on a date that was, or might have been, eaten by a chicken or a goat … It's laughable. But the hagiographies are riddled with details of this kind. So it simply doesn't have the symbolic value of a text that gets written on the basis of an initial loss.

A: On top of the materials that just happen to be lying around, Gabriel turns up every time Muhammad finds himself in a pickle.

H: There's another problem: historicization – since it's only through the Old Testament that we can get our bearings in relation to the events in the Qur'an.

A: We musn't forget that the Qur'an was written, on the one hand, in an atmosphere of intellectual affinity between Muhammad and the Nestorians of Arabia whose chief was Waraqa ibn Nawfal, and, on the other, in an atmosphere of war between Quraysh and the other Arab tribes. The Qur'an arose out of very complex conditions from an economic and political point of view. To say nothing of the conflict between Arabs and foreigners.

H: Meaning?

A: The conflicts between the tribes of Arabia would turn, later on, into struggles between Arabs and non-Arabs. Islam was on the side of the Jews at first, then against them later on; it was with Quraysh at first, then against them later on. The Ansar took the place of the Qurayshites … So the conditions in which the Revelation took place were extremely complicated. It was a world full of war and conflict. And 'Uthmān's move (burning those six versions of the Qur'an) was the height of the violence. Add to that the immense difference between the Meccan suras and the Medinan suras, as you mentioned.

H: Indeed, why are the Medinan suras so incredibly long? Logically, you could say the faculty of memory isn't called on in the same way. Only, how can you get your mind around the claim that the angel came back to say he'd keep going with the sura, which had been started but not finished?

A: The length differs and so does the content. To say nothing of the cancellation of one Qur'anic verse by another that replaces it. This issue of abrogation needs to be looked at again in greater depth. How is it that God, who is normally exempt from all error, reveals a verse only to then change it afterwards by declaring it null and void? If God is changeable, this means that he is not an absolute wellspring or authority. Such a thing was never seen before in the history of monotheism.

H: God cannot be 'a deceiver' or 'an evil *jinn*'. The Arab world is sorely lacking in a Cartesian revolution. Descartes introduced doubt as a method.

A: How come God changed his mind? 'And for whatever verse We abrogate or cast into oblivion, We bring a better or the like of it.'[20]

H: We'll actually be looking at those verses again. I might remind you that this issue of the *naskh*[21] had an economic basis, as has been said. The relevant verse begins like this: 'O believers, when you conspire with the Messenger, before your conspiring advance a freewill offering.' The Meccans protested, since they'd left their goods behind and lived in poverty in Medina, and the Medinese, offering the Meccans hospitality, didn't have an easy life. Having demanded a salary for Muhammad, in the face of the general outcry, Gabriel came back to rectify matters: 'Yet if you find not means, God is All-forgiving.'[22] The verse only lasted a *sāʿa min al-nahār*, an hour of the day.

A: God reveals a verse and then, after experimenting with it from a pragmatic point of view, realizes it isn't suitable and reveals another one. How are we to read this act?

H: And there's this other verse: 'O believers, fear God *ḥaqqa tuqātihi* (as He should be feared).'[23] When this verse was revealed, people voiced their bewilderment over the phrase *ḥaqqa tuqātihi* and asked Muhammad to explain its meaning to them. The verse was abrogated and it became: 'So fear God *mā istaṭaʿtum* (as far as you are able).'[24]

A: These references and commentaries are priceless. It's the Qur'an and Gabriel who are doing the thinking – not human beings.

H: And what's the sense of an utterance that isn't understood by the people to whom it's addressed? We find some pretty implausible commentaries. For instance: 'Move not thy tongue with it [in reading the Qur'an] to hasten it [the Revelation].'[25] Ibn Kathīr comments on these verses in the following fashion: 'God ordered Muhammad to listen to the Revelation and made him promise to keep it in his heart. And so, Muhammad was able to repeat it exactly as he had received it.' Al-Qurṭubī writes that Sufyān moved his lips exactly like the Prophet did. And Ibn 'Abbās says: 'I moved my lips just as the Prophet had done.' As for Ṭabarī, he interprets the verse like this: 'We are going to memorize it for you' (*fa innā sanaḥfaẓuhu 'alayka*). In the view of Ibn Kathīr and Ṭabarī, Muhammad didn't even understand the sense of what he was saying.

A: This means that Muhammad had no connection with what he was uttering. He was a simple *nāqil*.[26] All these commentaries and interpretations reinforce the extremely political sense of the Revelation. Muhammad repeats everything word for word so the Arabs won't accuse him of inventing what he's saying. Don't forget the legend that claims Muhammad couldn't read or write.

H: This political dimension merges with a psychological aspect. I've often wondered about the construction of the Arab family novel. Moses grew up in the palace of the pharoah and was literate. Why does the Arab decide that his mother, Hajar, was a slave, and that his prophet was an illiterate? What do we make of this debasement in the construction of origins?

A: We need to put Islam in its historical context. First, early Islam was Jewish and so did not criticize the Jews – at least not in its initial stages. Second, there were several prophets in Arabia. Muhammad and Khadīja went on to create a different model of prophecy. Hence the insistence on the illiteracy of Muhammad, who merely repeated God's words without moving his lips. We're faced with a completely new model: speaking a divine utterance that escapes the human. Which is a way of telling the Arabs not to resist this utterance which doesn't come from Muhammad, but from God. Muhammad isn't lying or inventing.

H: Those who now opt to read it as a divine text talk about the modernity of the Qur'an's style: the way there's no linearity, so you can start any verse of any sura anywhere … Some say it's a text that recalls the modernity of Joyce.

A: I gave a paper on the issue in the 1980s at the Collège de France and I called it 'The Qur'anic Text and Writing Agendas'. I said it was a prose poem that was open on all sides. The writing of the Qur'an represents a revolution, as you can start with any verse and end with any other verse. It's like a wide-open garden that you can enter from any side. In that sense, it's extraordinarily modern. But, should we attribute a literary aspect to a divine text?

H: I remember that once, when I wanted to talk about the lack of linearity in the Qur'an, I did so in Ponge-like terms ('The original storm that roars inside us'). Now, I ask this question: is the disruption in the writing proof of its divine origin? Does the literary aspect suffice to define a text as divine? Is it the message we should judge or is it the style?

A: There is no structure in the Qur'an. In that sense, it's more modern than Joyce's *Ulysses*. There is no linearity, either. It's a volcano that explodes all over the place. You can pick it up at any one spot. But what we need to do today is make a critical study of the Text as it is. Are we bold enough to do that?

H: We'll follow up with this issue about memory. The Qur'an is spoken of as a text revealed and passed on intact, not altered by human words. Well, can we – and in what way, if so? – preserve a text intact in a context of wars, fighting, deaths and periods of deep mourning?

A: And, on top of that, did the Revelation last for a period of twenty-three years? What kind of memory is it that can keep working like this for twenty-odd years? You can learn in a few days or a few weeks, but not twenty-three years!

H: The issue of memory takes on a crucial importance. I read that Muhammad sometimes forgot various verses and that Gabriel would come and remind him of them, that the caliph Umar wanted to reward the *hafazat al-Qur'an* (men who'd learnt the Qur'an by heart) but he drew a blank, since the men were either dead or were too caught up in wars of conquest and so had no way of being able to learn the Qur'an by heart.

A: Despite that fact, 'falsehood comes not to it from before it nor from behind it'.[27] The Muslim must believe and apply.

H: Reading the hagiographical texts, we come across a number of stories that are worth thinking about. Before his farewell pilgrimage, Muhammad spent a month with Gabriel revising the Qur'an.

A: That supports what we were saying. There's doubt about the Text itself. I'll go back to what I was saying a moment ago about the Revelation and memory so as to further refine it. Muhammad appears as another 'copy' of God. He copied God's word exactly as it is. In which case, he's master of nothing. Not even of the act of moving his lips. Who can say the word of God exactly as it is if not an individual who is like Him? This is why commentators have insisted on the manner in which the Qur'an was read. The prophet didn't act in any way. He was acted on.

H: 'To hasten it [the Revelation].'[28] Ṭabarī explains that it's the angel who memorized the verses in Muhammad's stead. The memory at work is Gabriel's. So at that point, what can the phrase 'the assembling of the Qur'an' signify?

A: A painful question, indeed.

H: Ṭabarī writes that Muhammad recited without grasping the sense of what he was saying. To underscore the divine aspect, they actually strip the individual of his cognitive, subjective and mental faculties.

A: The worst thing is that Muslims' attachment to this text is not an expression of any kind of awareness, but a defensive reaction in relation to their ignorance. Islam today is a reflection of today's Muslims. An indiscriminate ban on knowledge and not a defence of knowledge and learning.

H: Let's continue our reflections on the Text. What do we make of 'We have sent it down as an Arabic Qur'an'?[29] No language is pure. And we know now that several terms that feature in the Qur'an are not Arabic – for instance, *aṣṣirâṭ*.[30]

A: Those are terms that were Arabized. People may well have protested and asked, why not have a Qur'an in another language? Why did God opt for the Arab language? If they say the Qur'an is for Arabs, whereas the message is intended for the whole world, that's a contradiction.

H: The Arab language existed before Islam. But this genre of verse has permeated Arabs' memory. One of the best-known songs in the Arab world used to be 'The whole world speaks Arabic' (*il-'arḍ bititkallim 'arabī*).[31]

A: The Qur'an that came after the Arab language then comes first. It becomes the origin of the Arab language, when historically it's a second text. Poetry is earlier. But the Revelation took up such a lot of space that people forgot the language was already there well before Islam.

H: You've written some really beautiful things about the Arab language, which you've called an exploding bomb: 'the language of deflagration', a bomb exploding. Today, that language is being mangled, for we're seeing a corruption of the language in the interests of defending the Text. To cite one example, the verse on women says: *iḍrubūhunna*,[32] which means 'Hit them! (or 'Beat them!'). Well, modern commentators say the word *ḍaraba*[33] doesn't mean what it means.

A: It just goes to show that nothing is stable in itself. And once God is the ultimate sense, *ḍaraba* takes on another sense. Which means that the language itself is devoid of a basis. In order to save the Text, the Muslim allows himself to destroy the language.

H: The humanities teach us that the only truth there is is based on language. From the moment the community agrees to say 'this is a cup', the cup becomes a signifier for that community. That a word can no longer mean what it means is illustrated magnificently in *Alice in Wonderland*. Except that the world described there turns into one of primary processes, the world of dream, of madness.

A: Here, it's all about the very erasure of the individual in favour of a theory that stipulates that nothing can exist except through the will of God. Muslims call this 'external logic'. I'll take from the Qur'an the example of the fire that doesn't burn. Normally, traditionally, and until further notice, fires burn. Well, in the Qur'anic verse, the distinctiveness of fire comes in for a drubbing. The fire didn't burn Ibrahim (Abraham).[34] Why didn't the fire burn him? Because God transforms the essence of things. Which equals a sort of cancellation of reason. And when reason is cancelled, man allows himself to commit crimes and other misdemeanours, as Voltaire said.

H: In the case of Abraham, we could retort that we're dealing with a miracle. On the other hand, in the verse that asks men to beat their wives, there's no question of a miracle whatsoever.

A: You're right, as you've put your finger on the distortion of the language. We can, in fact, see fire as a courtesy of God's. In contrast, we can't apply that rule to the verb 'to beat'. What's more, if God doesn't like injustice, by definition and in all logic, why does he ask for women to be beaten? But if we take our reflection on non-logic further, Jonah was swallowed by a whale. Can a person survive in the belly of a whale?

H: These legends can be interpreted in terms of miracles: the prophet of God is protected by God.

A: Yes, but you have to believe in them. Actually, we shouldn't just stick to one or two examples, but reconsider the whole. In light of the whole, we can see this transformation of the essence of things more clearly. Man – every bit as much as the things of this world – loses his essence, his sense and his significance.

H: This clinging to the Text poses a real problem today, since people are in conflict with the Universal Declaration of Human Rights. Yet, instead of improving the status of women or working towards changing it by reflecting on the Text and its violence, they attack the language.

A: We need to deconstruct the logic of Islam from the inside, for it rests on the law of arbitrariness. From the point of view of that logic, humanity as idea and as representation just doesn't hold up. It's the very sense of existence that finds itself thus under attack. To say that things depend absolutely on the will of God is to allow the lie to become truth and fire to be turned into water. The essence of things is cancelled.

H: What you're saying is that there's only a human element if there's a linguistic structure. And the moment people attack the language, they attack the human. When a word is deprived of its meaning, when it no longer designates what it's supposed to designate, what's left?

A: We need to remember that Islam did not deny magic. When God wants to, He does what He likes. In the mind of the faithful, only God is capable of such effects. And so He is the only magician in existence. The transformation of Moses's stick into a snake, for instance, comes under magic. But in God's eyes, it's not a matter of magic, but of His capacity to create. 'When He decrees a thing, He but says to it "Be", and it is.'[35] Fakhr al-Dīn al-Rāzī[36] writes that, 'the people in the *sunna* accept that a magician can fly and turn a human being into an ass, and the other way around. In actual fact, it is God who accomplishes such things.'[37]

H: Such things, coming indeed under magical thinking, were consolidated by the Qur'an which also preaches the real existence of djinn.[38]

A: If you believe in the existence of genies, how can you believe in the human? And if fire doesn't burn, then water in no way slakes thirst.

H: In *Alice in Wonderland*, everything is possible. And the moment everything is possible, nothing is stable. Everything is commanded by the primary processes that prevail in the world of dream, fairytales and madness.

A: If it's not madness, strictly speaking, it comes pretty close. What is this doctrine in which magic becomes faith?

H: Speaking of *Alice in Wonderland*, Gilles Deleuze writes: 'The thing most deeply buried becomes manifest.' We could say the same about Islam. The fantasmagorical world, with its numberless houris, verbal communication via images of rivers of milk, genies who are each person's demons … rise to the surface again.

A: Exactly. And it's this imaginary realm we need to question, along with the language God uses: how can he talk about *jaḥīm*, *ṣadīd*, *ṣaqar*, *'adhāb*[39] and other words so cruel your mouth has trouble saying them? The Text says: '… so let them taste it – boiling water and pus, and other torments of the like kind coupled together.'[40] They've painted a picture of God as a torturer, who uses horrible words. The Text attests to the fact that, right up to the present day, Muslims have been unable to come up with a noble picture of God.

H: The idea of a vengeful God (*muntaqim*) contradicts the idea of the God of Mercy. *Al-baṭsh*[41] is a divine attribute. Here the language is a language of cruelty, violence and hatred.

Even sexuality is ranked more with control, possession and consummation than with some beautiful encounter that opens out into desire and the thrilling excitement one human being feels for another human being.

A: The language is very primitive, at times even vulgar. There are terms that are indecent. I've always wondered how a God could use terms like *inkaḥū*[42] of women?

H: There is indeed a certain crudity in the Qur'an when it comes to matters of sex. For example: 'And Mary, Imran's daughter, who guarded *farjahā*.'[43] Mustapha Safouan is right to raise the issue of the translation of the Qur'an into vernacular languages[44] because no Moroccan, Lebanese or Syrian … would dare say that particular verse in the vernacular. The Qur'an could have said guarded her soul (*nafsahā*) or her virginity (*'udhriyyatahā*). But when it comes to matters of sex, the terms and images that feature in the Qur'an are very crude. In the vernacular, some verses become, ethically and morally, impossible to say.

A: It's that same crudity that we also find in the images that serve to frighten those who refuse to follow the religious doctrine. How can God, symbol of mercy, speak in terms of *jaḥīm*?[45] These are very cruel terms. The Qur'anic verses strive to outdo each other in terms of savagery and violence:

> Surely those who disbelieve in Our signs – We shall certainly roast them at a Fire; as often as their skins are wholly burned, We shall give them in exchange other skins, that they may taste the chastisement.[46]

H: 'The deepest thing in man is the skin', as Paul Valéry once said.

A: The Muslims of the day didn't know that.

H: On the one hand, the Qur'an invites them to eat well and to copulate; on the other, torture is lying in wait for anyone who doesn't submit to the injunctions of the Text. So the wrath of God descends on whoever isn't tempted by eating, drinking and copulating as their rewards. Eating, drinking and copulating, such as the Qur'an portrays them, define the reader as being all about basic consumption. Everything is caught up in the register of the primary – the present every bit as much as the future.

A: The individual's life on Earth is a pale representation of a very wan copy of life in paradise. The Muslim must live on Earth in anticipation of what will be in the afterlife. The Earth being but a passage, true pleasure is what's on offer in paradise. That's why sexuality is so important in these texts.

H: Let's go back to the issue of language in the Qur'anic Text. When the Qur'an addresses Muslims, in the afterlife, saying, 'Eat and drink in peace [with wholesome appetite]',[47] it makes the future immediately accessible through language. Paradise is not in some future time, or to come. It becomes immediate through the use of the present tense. And so, the distant phenomenon becomes close, incredibly present, through the use of the grammatical form of the present tense. It doesn't say: 'You will eat and drink in peace [with wholesome appetite].' Hearing that verse, the Muslim sees himself in the process of satisfying his urges. Everything becomes possible, just like in *Alice in Wonderland*.

A: We're dealing here with a linguistic structure that makes the phenomenon possible. There's a transfer of one meaning to a different meaning. When fire no longer burns but turns to water, we're dealing with a second meaning. And that's where the great complexity lies, since Muslims, in general, insist on a word's literality. From that moment on, everything becomes true.

H: Well, in *Poetics*, Aristotle talks about language being 'seasoned', referring to metaphor. Language can't be thought about without metaphor.

A: When it is written that 'He sat Himself upon the throne',[48] people try to resolve this question: how can he sit when he doesn't have a body? The Mu'tazilites tried to solve the question of anthropomorphism. But most people say: 'He sat Himself *bilā kayf* ("without asking how").'[49]

H: That's the Asharite position.

A: It's also the reasoning of the Sunnis. Once Muslims all became adepts of the *sunna*, the language did not emerge unscathed. The entire language ends up in a difficult position. Paradise, linguistically speaking, is a metaphor. But for Muslims, paradise is a reality. If you take an object – a cushion, say – and you ask a Muslim, he'll tell you that the object is a cushion, God willing. And with God's will, it can turn into water or be transformed into something else again. Reason, intellect and the faculty of judgement comply with divine will.

H: Well, a thing exists in my representation because it has existed in reality. This is known as the judgement of existence.

A: We can say, then, that the problem lies there. If it's belief that decides everything, the judgement of existence is invalid by definition. Now, if this was just an individual problem, we could talk about the suffering of one individual. But in our case, the problem involves whole societies. How can you insist that individuals are all the same when even machines are different from each other? In the eyes of the law, we are all identical. If I want to go on a fast, or pray in a different way, or not pray, I have no right to say or do so. My freedom as an individual is taken away by a legal system that interferes in everything and imposes its rules, its rites, on the whole set of individuals.

H: You're talking here about mass madness and the difference between belief and truth. The judgement of existence takes care of meaning. Here, there is no meaning.

A: It's all about the cancelling of the original meaning and its replacement by another meaning. And so the conquests of the Muslims are a sort of *Alice in Wonderland*.

H: I understand what you're saying as this: the unlimited – or limitless – becomes Event and this passes for History. No one has ever acknowledged this particular problem.

A: There's a kind of madness when it comes to belief, a madness that's vindicated.

H: If you understand 'I, God, absolute truth, am speaking', in the light of abrogation, you can't avoid the following question: how can what He says be irresolute, changeable, not stable? And in light of what you're saying about the cancellation of thinking by the religious structure of Islam, I'm now gauging the extent to which the *cogito* has been lacking in the Arab world. Meaning, the capacity of an 'I' that doubts, reflects, thinks, judges, draws conclusions …

A: For there to be a *cogito*, there needs first to be a human being. I recall what *Shāfiʿī* said: 'Whoever speaks of the Qur'an is in error, even if he speaks the truth.' Even if he speaks the truth, what he says is erroneous. And if he defends his opinion, he gets attacked. The image that springs to mind is of a magic box in which each person cancels out the other. Every individual can in God's name exterminate the other. Life in Islam rests on this cancellation of the other.

H: In Deleuzian terms, this is a cancellation of the 'other-structure'. So why have people talked about the challenge of the Qur'an? The content is a web of already existing legends and of laws. The extremely beautiful language was recorded magnificently in pre-Islamic poetry. Where's the challenge?

A: The Ancients, such as Al-Jāḥiẓ, refused to concede that there was a linguistic challenge. And yet, to escape reprisals, they used to talk about the inimitability of the content.

H: We raised that in the first volume of *Violence and Islam*. All revolutions have failed in the Arab world. It may be that socioeconomic, Marxist-Leninist analyses aren't enough. Freud needs to make his entrance in the Arab world so as to throw light on this clinging of the individual to a religious structure full of contradictions and paradoxes. He loves it as he loves himself.

A: What happened in the very early days of Islam is being played out again now. Let's take the case of Turkey and Erdoğan's cancellation of civil society. Every construction, everything that was built up over a century of secularism, has been cast aside. Erdoğan has swept away a modern society in order to return to a primitive structure. And the world isn't protesting about it. He has staged a *coup d'état* against modernity and against human beings.

H: But the West is also contributing to this eternal return.

A: Of course. The West has soldiers who are ready to defend its interests. Before, Europe fought the Muslims.

Now, it goes along with the Salafists and the obscurantism they peddle for the sake of its interests.

H: Arab intellectuals find themselves faced with a thorny problem. As readers of Marcel Mauss, Durkheim, Freud … who all saw religion as an extension of totemism, they remain baffled by the verse 'God … who has not begotten, and has not been begotten,'[50] which cancels the idea that religion stems from totemism. How can people talk about religion as an extension of totemism and not question the Islamic vision?

A: The separation between Church and State allows us to discuss the bases of religiosity, its foundations, its history, its doctrines … Well, that doesn't apply to Islam, which seems to say: you have to accept and not discuss.

H: To say that Islam is not an extension of totemism is to do away with any feeling of guilt. How can you avoid guilt in the construction of social cohesion? How can you think of a civilization without guilt?

A: To feel guilt, you have first to admit you're at fault. Islam turned up with perfection. There is no fault or sin for there to be any guilt. Besides, Islam eliminated the notion of Christian sin. In its religious construction, all faults lie with the other, namely the unbeliever, the infidel. As for the Muslim, his sins and his faults are considered exclusively from the point of view of Islam. And his relation to the other occurs only through Islam. He is judged for his deviations in regard to the precepts of his religion and not in regard to the rules and laws of the world. To say that he is seen exclusively from inside Islam means he has no connection to the ontological issues of other human beings.

H: You say that religious doctrine has helped reinforce projection on the part of the Muslim. Instead of accepting fault, he projects onto the other what he can't accept in himself.

A: Absolutely. We note moreover that in the long history of the Arabs, no one has ever admitted any error whatsoever. And when – and it's rare – people say they've made mistakes, like Nasser did after the defeat of 1967, the people opposed his resignation. He himself, instead of insisting on resigning, stayed in power. In his subconscious, he was Muslim. And if we leave the world of politics for the world of literature, the art of autobiography, as an example, is pretty meagre. With such meagreness, no author says he's committed or made mistakes and consequently seeks to analyse his inadequacies, his weaknesses … in short, the things that make us human.

H: I think you're the only person who's written:

Umar, 'Alī, 'Uthmān, the first companion,
Mu'āwiya, Yazīd
Abū Ṭālib,
and Abū Lahab,
are still alive
and their sons are copies.
From the beginning of our history not one of us has had a taste of death.[51]

A: That is in actual fact the whole issue of murder in Islam. Islam has produced a society in which thought is attacked and the 'I' is fought against, except in the pathological sense: 'I am the best! I am the greatest!' …

H: You mean: an 'I' expressing an 'ego' who revels in narcissism. The verse that refers to us as 'the best nation'[52] has certainly fuelled this narcissistic dimension which, all things considered, remains problematic. I'm thinking again of your essay on the impact of Salafism on Muslims' subjectivity.

A: I wrote that the individual ego had no arena in which it could move around, reject, repudiate, accept, doubt or believe. For embracing another vision of the world or declaring your impiety means exclusion from the community. While a human being's freedom makes for the essence of that human being, doctrine condemns him to renounce what makes for his essence, his worth and his being. I repeat, man is born into this culture like a full-stop in a book that is the community or the nation. How can an individual strait-jacketed by the Text create, or lay claim to, a creative ego?

H: '... and when thou threwest, it was not thyself that threw, but God threw.'[53] The individual finds himself dispossessed even of his actions. Where is human responsibility?

A: The philosopher Al-Fārābī[54] said: 'Every being existing in a machine delegates his self to others and every being existing in himself has his self at his own command.' That's the reason why I spoke about the 'uncritical follower' (*al-tābi'*). Instead of sounding the innermost depths of his soul, he dissolves into doctrine and rites, without ever questioning them.

H: He can't, in that context, have a conversation with himself.

A: How can he have a conversation with himself if he only places himself as *tābi'*? He mimics the prophet's companions as perfect or accomplished men. And these perfect or accomplished people are followed uncritically by the majority of Muslims. Well, the validity of a fact or truth can't be measured quantitatively. And so we can say the Muslim lives in 'two prisons', to use the expression of the poet Al-Ma'arrī:[55] the prison of orthodox, traditionalist interpretation, and the prison created by the forfeiture of his own ego, his self, and so, of his subjectivity.

H: When guilt is missing, perversion promotes psychopathy. In our work on today's extremism, which is now known as radicalization, we need to think things through in light of this cancellation of the ego and the 'I', and the way the individual is dispossessed of his own actions. It's a very complex and very difficult project. Tricky. The religious context doesn't explain everything. But that factor must not be disregarded. Especially since today's extremism is a return to what already existed, and so to what was brewing away in the murky depths and is now resurfacing.

A: We ask questions, raise queries and we don't have absolute answers. But you have to admit that Arabs are now almost totally oblivious to societal demands, modernity and respect for human rights and their own right to plurality and difference.

H: We have two kinds of Arab individuals: those who know the Greeks, Hegel, Lacan, Durkheim, Freud … and who aren't about to read Muslim and Bukhārī, who have no ideas, or the imams who know Bukhārī and Muslim but are never going to throw themselves into the philosophical or anthropological or psychoanalytical corpus of today's humanities. That, it seems to me, is one of the great crises of the Arab world. On the one hand, generations of francophones and anglophones in total ignorance of these texts that have the force of law, and, on the other, *fuqahā'*[56] who are out of sync with modernity and with societal changes. Our misfortune is that the laws of the city are still based on Muslim and Al-Bukhārī.

A: And so, on the *fiqh*[57] and power. The *fiqh* is bound up with power. It's just the other side of power. That said, and even though the Text remains the primary reference, we might note that the arts that have evolved in the Arab and Muslim world are those that have no frame of reference in the past: namely drawing, film, painting, architecture and theatre. All the domains that don't refer to the Islamic corpus as a benchmark have evolved. This proves just how extremely solid a shackle Islam is. If God is the sole creator, how can you expect him not to be against the arts?

H: I gladly adopt Assia Djebbar's phrase: 'So vast the prison!'

A: Abū l-'alā' al-Ma'arrī summed it up when he said: 'The inhabitants of the Earth are of two sorts: those who have brains but no religion, and those who have religion but no brains.' Believing in Islam, its doctrine and precepts, implies the negation of thought. From the moment that everything is in the Qur'an, the Muslim is compelled to read the Qur'an so as to both know the world and how to conduct himself. I repeat, all we're doing is raising questions without claiming to provide answers.

H: A moment ago you raised the issue of anthropomorphism that once sparked a great debate between the Mu'tazilites, defenders of absolute transcendence, and the Asharites, who opted for the *bilā kayf*.[58] In light of our exchange, I'm finally realizing that, when the Mu'tazilites tried to resolve the question of anthropomorphism – by resorting to metaphor, allegory and other figures of style – they started with the Text and they stayed with the Text. Despite their enormous audacity (saying, for example, that the Qur'an was created) and the power of their reasoning, they actually shored up the doctrine by providing more bases for it and giving it more consistency, instead of questioning it.

A: The Mu'tazilites said the Qur'an was created to preserve the divine essence, so that this essence remained one and indivisible. While the Muslims were defending the Text out of sheer belief, the Muʿtazilites were arguing the case for the greatness of the Text by resorting to reasoning.

H: When we were adolescents, we were proud to learn that Abū l-Hudhayl al-ʿAllāf[59] could use reasoning to convert hundreds of individuals to Islam.

A: Having been a miracle through belief, the Qur'an became a miracle through recourse to reasoning. That's one reason why Muʿtazilitism – in the history of Muslim thought – is a sort of decadence. I wrote in *Al-Thābit wa l-Mutaḥawwil*[60] that Muʿtazilitism complicated the issue of Islam by turning belief into an affair of pure intellect and pure reasoning.

H: I prefer Kierkegaard, who said that 'faith starts where reason stops'. This leads me to say that we're not dealing here with faith, but with the manufacture of a story. We're not deconstructing faith but the manufacture of a problematic corpus that has the force of history.

A: In that case, let's say that, from a poetic, intellectual and philosophical point of view, Islam is finished. And yet, it continues to rule politically.

4

Saqīfa: Power in a Tizzy

H: We might recall that, before the advent of Islam, the Ka'ba was a place of pilgrimage, for pilgrims of all religions. It was the year 8 Hijra (AD 630) that Muhammad, having become extremely powerful after his military successes, banned idolaters, Jews and Christians from making the pilgrimage. So it was in the year 8 Hijra that the Ka'ba became definitively Muslim.

A: And yet, pagan rites didn't abandon the Ka'ba. Quite the opposite. Muhammad dressed the Ka'ba up as Muslim, but didn't basically change anything. The Ka'ba preserved all its rites, and so remained pagan. Muhammad Islamized it only from the point of view of the *shar'*.

H: I meant that the act of banning access to the Ka'ba to all non-Muslims attests to its military, political and financial power.

A: And it's the same as if you took a house and decorated it differently, and then you become the owner.

H: Before he died, Muhammad made the farewell pilgrimage (*ḥajjat al-wadāʿ*) on 25 *dhū al-ḥijja* of the year 10 Hijra (23 March 602). At the time of this pilgrimage, the Hashemites (Muhammad's family and clan) were named as possessors of the Sacred Word, since it was ʿAlī who was to be chosen to lead the prayer.

A: Except that Muhammad's two companions, Umar and Abū Bakr, turned their noses up at his last wishes, expressed while he was on the pilgrimage.

H: And it was while he was on this pilgrimage that he uttered this sentence, which you've often commented on and criticized: 'Today, I have perfected [*'atmamtu*] your religion for you.'

A: You have to follow through: *wa raḍītu lakum al-'islāma dīnan* (I have accepted Islam as a religion for you).

H: This gives us pause for thought about the status of Muhammad's word. There is the *ḥadīth*, which is the word of the prophet of Islam, and there's the *ḥadīth qudsī*, according to which it's God who's speaking through Muhammad's mouth. In the sentence ('I have perfected ...'), who is the 'I' who is speaking? Is it God? Or is it Muhammad? We see the elimination of the boundary between the human and the divine.

A: It's God who is speaking through the mouth of Muhammad. Here, we're dealing with the word of God. As if it was another kind of Revelation.

H: This prompts us to raise the issue of the *ḥadīth qudsī*. Muhammad speaks in God's stead. I think it's the first time in the history of monotheism that a God speaks through the mouth of a human being or that a human being expresses himself while being God. Gabriel vanishes as an intermediary.

A: Indeed, it's like the ancient priest who spoke the words of the gods. So, the *ḥadīth qudsī* could be seen as a copy of the Greek tradition. It's the word of an oracle.

H: Despite the sacred side of the *ḥadīth*, every hagiographer or every group was to reproduce it in its own way. Which gives us multiple different versions of the same *ḥadīth*. For instance: 'I have left you two things', says Muhammad, 'which will keep you from going astray: the Qur'an and my family.' You find that version among the Shiites, in Tirmidhī and in Ṭabarī. On the other hand, in other versions, it goes 'I have left you the Qur'an and the *sunna*.' The word 'family' disappears. The narratives are contradictory, and the different versions very different. And the *'an'ana*[1] doesn't really help in putting together a historiographical work.

A: I suggest we only discuss the object agreed on by the different groups or the different schools. We need to give priority to the narrative that has unanimous backing.

H: But we also need to point out the contradictions and say that there are sometimes as many versions as there are individuals.

A: The versions differ from each other and contradict each other. On top of that, they steer well clear of any scientific approach. Each individual wove a story according to his imagination. What he had to say was strictly linked to his family and tribal affiliations, his economic interests, and so on. So, it's the individual who is the primary source and not the Text.

H: We are in fact faced with a question of methodology. Even if we opt for the versions common to the different groups, we'd still have to point out the contradictions. Because this shows, as you've just indicated, that History has gone through a set of narratives that are non-objective, since they relate to the interests of the people who've manufactured or composed them.

A: If we focused on all the contradictions, we'd never get the job done. The complexities are numerous, even if we take one version that all Muslims agreed on. Consequently, we are going to start with this response of Muhammad's that had unanimous backing. When he was asked, while he was sick and in bed, to choose the person who would wash his body after he died, he replied: '*Ahlī*' (people in my family). He didn't name anyone.

H: Did *Ahlī* mean 'Alī or his uncle Ibn 'Abbās or both? Since you could be forgiven for thinking that this response is along the same lines as singling out 'Alī to read the Qur'an during the final pilgrimage.

A: This word *Ahlī*, which everyone vouches for, proves that corruption was the basis and foundation of Islamic society, that is to say that it was the Quraysh tribe that manufactured Islamic society; and it shows, by the same token, how very fragile its construction was. Muhammad united the tribes. But the tribal spirit remained very powerful regardless. He himself was very attached to the Banū Hāshim, his family.

H: We read that Muhammad foiled an assassination attempt organized by Abū Bakr, Umar and Abū 'Ubayda ibn al-Jarrāḥ. For when he singled out 'Alī to read the Qur'an, Abū Bakr, Umar and Abū 'Ubayda were frightened that 'Alī would seize the reins of power. Ṭabarī relates how the three men plotted against Muhammad and drew up a pact. Hence the verse on the deceit and hypocrisy of people who were close to Muhammad.[2]

A: When we read the hagiographical works, we also see how the prophet of Islam was, himself, used. He became a means of access to power and the exercise of power. In fact, it wasn't just a matter of using Muhammad, but of using Islam in general.

H: When you say 'using', we should specify 'by Abū Bakr and Umar'. But let's take it one step at a time. At first, Abū Bakr was sad when Muhammad chose 'Alī to read the Qur'an at the Ka'ba. Sad because he saw himself divested of a noble task. And Muhammad replied: 'The message of God can only be read by a Hashemite.'[3] As the religious and the political were not dissociated, this was a way of singling out 'Alī as his successor.

A: Yes, we find that in Ṭabarī. Muhammad said: 'Summon 'Alī' or 'Call 'Alī'. Aïsha said: 'Call Abū Bakr', that is, her father. Aïsha, says Ṭabarī, was very quick to put forward her father. But if Muhammad chose his family, that was because he preferred them to any other Muslims. This preference for his family was later exploited by Abū Bakr and Umar, who gave the term a broader meaning, after Muhammad's death, so as to rule out the Ansar. They said: 'We deserve the caliphate, as we are the closest to Muhammad.' 'Alī didn't fail to point out the contradiction there, claiming that Umar and Abū Bakr were using this argument in neglect of 'Alī, who was the closest to Muhammad since he was a cousin and son-in-law.

H: Their argument backfired on them.

A: All this proves that it was a well-prepared and incredibly violent *coup d'état*. Saqīfa was an assassination of the Ansar. But well before the *coup d'état*, Muhammad was abandoned before he died and before he was buried. And his companions from way back refused to respond to his plea when, as he lay there dying, he wanted to write a will.

H: Aïsha, Muhammad's wife, her father Abū Bakr, Ḥafṣa, the co-wife, and her father Umar organized everything and saw to it that Muhammad didn't leave a will, as we read in a book by Hela Ouardi.[4] Abū Bakr abandoned Muhammad in a critical state and left for Al-Sunh, a long way from Medina, so as to ensure that the treasure trove was nicely hidden away. During that time, Muhammad was clamouring for something to write with. But his pleas were to no avail.

A: Saqīfa wasn't just a *coup d'état* against the Ansar, it was against Muhammad himself.

H: 'Bring me a quill and an inkwell', he clamoured. The only answer he got was this sentence: 'The Messenger of God *kāna yahjūru*'. How are we supposed to interpret that word, *yahjūru*?

A: 'He was raving.'

H: Then, can we say that his nearest and dearest accused him of raving so as to stop him from leaving a will? After all, only a person of sane mind can draw up a will. What violence vis-à-vis their prophet!

A: Indeed. It showed great violence towards a person who wanted to record his last wishes before dying. This accusation emanated, what's more, from the people closest to him. It's evidence of a categorical rejection of a will. Second, Muhammad was known to be an *'ummī*.[5] How could he write? This request to draw up a will destroyed an image built up over several years – the image of Muhammad as an illiterate. It's extremely likely that the delirium was also a construction designed to safeguard the image of a man who said everything through a divine voice. Which leads us to have doubts about every single construction relating to the person of Muhammad.

H: This request to draw up a will was made when Muhammad was extremely weak from his illness. People mention pleurisy. But there are several stories based on the hypothesis that he was poisoned. It's said that he had a blackout, that the family members present took advantage of this to dab a remedy at the corners of his mouth, and that he was furious when he woke up and he demanded that everyone take some.

A: In Arabic, his illness is called *dhāt al-janab*. He ordered everyone to drink the remedy. This has led researchers to put forward several hypotheses on the climate of suspicion that reigned in Muhammad's household. Hence, perhaps, the desire to leave a will relating to the succession.

H: What *is* commonly accepted is that Muhammad's death took place in AD 632. But Ṭabarī stipulates that this date isn't definite and that it was chosen later on. In fact, nothing is definite, neither the date of his birth nor the date of his death. And even the claim that he was forty years old at the time of the Revelation could just be a traditional device.

A: I'm going to go even further. The story was written late in the day. Hence the multiple versions of the same event. But when it comes to the will, the versions may vary, but the meaning remains the same: 'You won't go wrong after my death if I leave you a will.'

H: That's doubly interesting: first, because it de-idealizes the picture we've painted for ourselves of the prophet's family; and second, because this story – whether real or fictional – is a way of expressing Muhammad's distress. When he was told he was suffering from pleurisy, his reaction was: 'God cannot give His prophet such a monstrous illness.' I stress that 'cannot' on the part of a prophet who himself taught his community the story of Job, but who, at the same time, voices Jesus' cry 'Why have you forsaken me?'. While wanting to be above the human condition, Muhammad's helplessness is that of a human being.

A: The prophet's family and those close to him were sacralized or idealized. But, it's from this same family that the attacks came. Refusing to record his last wishes is a serious act of betrayal. In his illness, Muhammad wanted to wed his fate to that of the community. Clamouring for a will, he says: '*lan tuḍillū ba'da Muhammad*' (You will not take the wrong path after Muhammad). All the reference books vouch for this version. Ṭabarī notes that there was disagreement and conflict among his closest relations.

H: But before Muhammad's death, there was already a conflict over the succession. Ibn al-Abbās questioned 'Alī on the subject: 'Did he leave a will for us?' 'Alī didn't dare ask Muhammad.

A: Actually, 'Alī didn't want to ask Muhammad, for he told himself: 'If ever he refused, all would be irrevocably lost.'

H: Everyone was after power.

A: But Muhammad asked them to look after the Ansar. He said: 'Al-Anṣār have my full confidence.'

H: From a symbolic point of view, the Ansar were the closest.

A: That's what the Qurayshites didn't want to see and categorically rejected. And so conflict was inevitable, and this, from the very beginning. The caliphate arose in this atmosphere of extreme violence towards Muhammad and the Ansar. Umar showed draconian violence and great intransigence: cutting off hands, beheading, crucifying, burning … The story of Umar's threatening to burn down Faṭima's house if she kept on refusing to swear allegiance to Abū Bakr is well known.

H: Reading the hagiographies, we become aware of the great political strategy Abū Bakr and Umar worked out to grab power. When Muhammad died, Umar feigned disbelief, saying that Muhammad had merely absented himself, just as Moses had.

A: Pure histrionics.

H: That's also the conclusion of Al-Wāqidī, who raises the issue of Abū Bakr's absence while Muhammad lay dying. They think this set-up was a way of stalling for time so they could organize the succession properly. And they relate that when Abū Bakr came back from Medina and discovered that Muhammad had died, he said the now famous verse: 'Muhammad is naught but a Messenger; Messengers have passed away before him.'[6] But we read in Ṭabarī that Umar and a few of Muhammad's companions admitted they'd never heard that verse, didn't know it and were hearing it for the first time. What do we make of the story of a verse revealed after Muhammad's death?

A: There were, it's true, several quarrels about the Qur'anic verses, notably between Aïsha and 'Uthmān.

H: With Aïsha saying, for instance, that the sura known as 'The Factions' [Apartments] initially contained a hundred verses, whereas 'Uthmān's version only kept seventy-three. In the case that interests us here, only Abū Bakr remembered this verse after Muhammad's death.

A: The consequences are serious, in either case. Because in all logic it makes you have doubts about the entire Qur'anic

Text. Political and economic interests created a world in which narratives served either to defend those interests or to incriminate opponents. A verse that no one knew is an example that speaks for itself.

H: Hela Ouardi wonders about the absence of a doctor at Muhammad's bedside as he lay sick and dying. Medicine existed at the time. Abū Bakr, for instance, was treated by three doctors, and Umar by six.

A: The events that occurred during Muhammad's illness and after his death clearly show non-respect for his person, and even extreme aggressiveness towards him.

H: To the point of forgetting about him and leaving him for three days without a burial because of the power struggle. They say the smell of the corpse became unbearable, that it 'infested the place'.

A: So I say again: leaving him to die and abandoning him in order to settle issues of power is disgraceful. It demands that Muslims reflect on the fact and analyse it. What do we make of the fact that his closest companions abandoned him like that?

H: The texts speak of a *mise en scène*, verses cropping up out of nowhere and a great deal of scheming and deftness in taking power from 'Alī and the Ansar.

A: The Ansar were excluded even though they favoured peace and opposed discord and war. They proposed that power be shared between themselves and the Qurayshites. They said: 'Let's choose one emir from among ourselves, and another from among you.' But they came up against the opposition of Abū Bakr and of Umar.

H: That's where we can really gauge the magnitude of the unease left by the lack of a will.

A: In Muhammad's lifetime, the question never came up, since he had all authority. After his death, the Ansar didn't want the management of the city-state to be the exclusive right of a single group. Umar and Abū Bakr didn't oppose the Ansar alone, but also their cousins the Hashemites, saying the latter couldn't hold prophecy and power concurrently. The first caliphate, then, happened in this atmosphere of discord and extreme violence. To say nothing of Umar's proposal: that the choice of a caliph be made solely by the bigwigs.

H: You mean the people, the grassroots Muslims, were excluded?

A: The choice fell to the notables and the elite, and not to the Muslims as a whole. This split had disastrous consequences, namely the division of the Muslims into two clans. One party with the caliph imposed by violence, and another that lost everything.

H: A double exclusion, then: of the Ansar and of the people of Quraysh.

A: The chief of the Ansar, Sa'd, refused to swear allegiance to Abū Bakr and died without pledging fealty. His life was spared not out of respect for his rank and age, but solely to avoid fuelling the anger of his family and friends. It was very strategic. People would say, later on, that the caliphate of Abū Bakr was an aberration.

H: Yet despite that, the image that spread everywhere is of two disinterested men, two perfect companions of the prophet's, two role models for the community. And even if, in the history books, they talk about the cupidity of 'Uthmān, who became the third caliph and who was assassinated for emptying the state coffers, Abū Bakr and Umar are always presented as great men of integrity.

A: All Muhammad's companions who became caliphs were inordinately rich. Their fortunes grew as they notched up conquests.

H: Ṭabarī talks about Umar's greed, on display one day when he was leading prayers but kept getting the recital of a sura wrong because his mind was focused on the sum of money he was about to get from *Shām*.[7] Umar was thinking about his financial deals even during prayers.

A: And before dying, Abū Bakr said to his daughter Aïsha: 'See how my fortune has grown since I became caliph. And give it back to the Muslims.'

H: Abū Bakr was named Al-Ṣiddīq.[8] From the moment Muhammad singled him out as the Truthful One, the Muslim mind couldn't help but set him up in that position. That's why no one has ever looked into his morality or his ethics.

A: That's plausible. He certainly exploited his relationship with Muhammad and his closeness to him.

H: It's even said that Umar – who wasn't exactly a shining example of asceticism – called him to order one day. That's a way of telling us that Islam hadn't tamed the driven side of man.

A: All the hagiographers agree that the first Muslim state was founded on well-organized violence, the effect of which was the exclusion of the Ansar. But today we should insist on the fact that there was a certain exploitation of Muhammad as a reference that was not religious, but ideological, the aim being to defend the foundation of a politico-religious society.

H: You're right to talk about a 'politico-religious society' because, even to the present day, we speak of the caliphs as *rāshidūn*.[9] People praise their religiousness but forget the political dimension.

A: That being the case, if Abū Bakr and Umar hadn't seized the reins of power, would the continuity of the first Muslim society have been saved? Saqīfa was virtually a military *coup d'état*.[10] And the proof is that the first founders continue to govern to this very day.

H: So that's all about the genius of Abū Bakr and Umar.

A: Umar more than Abū Bakr. But to get back to what we were saying a moment ago, they were closest to the prophet and, as a result, closest to the will of God. It's for this reason that there was a conflict over the meaning of the word 'close'. Who is the closest? 'Alī and his group, or Abū Bakr and his supporters?

H: While it could have a symbolic meaning, in this context the word 'close' has a political significance.

A: The state was founded on a political and economic interpretation of Islam. From the beginning, Islam was defined as *dīn wa dunyā*.[11] Which helped the Qurayshites create a model of governance that drew on Muhammad's relationship to God. The caliph thereby becomes God's caliph.

H: A model of governance that is connected to heaven, but doesn't relinquish the pleasures of life on Earth, including the enjoyment of power?

A: The founders exploited religion instead of submitting to it. In their hands, prophecy became a sword. That's why the war between Muslims has never ceased. During the fifty years that followed Muhammad's death up to the arrival of the Umayyads, violence was witnessed on a daily basis. Umar died assassinated, 'Uthmān died assassinated, 'Alī died assassinated and it's said that Abū Bakr was poisoned.

H: But as they were Muhammad's companions, they, too, have enjoyed the same privileges: they remain untouchable. Today, we know that 'Uthmān committed many injustices in relation to the people, but he is no less revered, just like the other early caliphs.

A: Between the caliphs themselves, there was a lust for murder. For example, Umar's violence towards 'Alī, which we've already mentioned. Whoever didn't submit to orders was exterminated, beheaded, burned, tortured ... Umar was known for his inflexibility and his intolerance.

H: And Abū Bakr, whom the hagiographers present as a fragile person, too tender-hearted, is the man who launched the cycle of conquests by leading a war known as *ridda* (against apostacy).

A: It wasn't really about waging war against apostates, but against those who refused to pay tribute after Muhammad's death. So it was an economic war. We need to remember, though, that there were people who rose up against totalitarian power. 'Alī was less violent. He said: 'Do not kill a single child, do not kill a single woman!'

H: And yet, after the death of his wife Faṭima, he gave his daughter Umayma, who was only ten years old, to Umar, who was very old, for a large sum of money. He also married 'Uthmān's daughter, who took the place of her aunt Fātima. That's another form of violence. But getting back to our theme: Muhammad invented a God and a Gabriel who corresponded to his desires and who fulfilled his desires.

A: Absolutely. And Umar and Abū Bakr used Muhammad and his God to build a political empire. Saqīfa illustrates that fact perfectly.

H: Islam imposed itself as a religion by the sword. And the foundation of the society, after the death of Muhammad, followed the same principle.

A: Yes. Islam is not a preaching religion. We might sum it up like this: 'I am the new religion. Welcome to whoever believes in it and woe betide whoever does not believe in it.'

H: We've touched on the hypothesis that Muhammad died through poisoning. Does that hypothesis argue in favour of the murder of the founder? Does it really manage to introduce the issue of murder in Islam?

A: I think that Judaism had an influence on Islam, that there's a definite similarity in terms of the law, the revival of a pre-biblical imagination, etc. But it's the tribal, political and economic aspect, not the spiritual aspect, that holds sway in Islam. On top of that, we mustn't lose sight of the other act of violence, namely the way in which Muhammad was torn from the bosom of his Hashemite community only to be treated as nothing more than a tribal chief.

H: In the myth described in *Totem and Taboo*, the murder of the father required solidarity and alliance between the brothers, who rebelled because they felt hard done by. Their impotence made them stick together. Well, in the context of

Islam, it wasn't an act of solidarity on the part of brothers to reverse the place of the father, but an act of betrayal. Something unheroic.

A: The founder wasn't killed like Moses or Jesus. But he was 'assassinated' in a different way. First, his friends left his corpse unburied. They were supposed to bury him first as a sign of loyalty. They literally abandoned him over political issues. Second, they took the power of his family and handed it to a rival family. And third, they imposed the caliphate by the sword and not by elections or choice.

H: Freud wrote that Islam was a copy of Judaism in which what was missing was the murder of the religion's founder.[12] Well, it's based on the principle of death that discourse can turn into the myth of language, according to Michel de Certeau. Murder signifies the appearance of the feeling of guilt and the emergence of culture. Without murder, we remain in admiration and in awe of the all-powerful or omnipotent, as we say in psychoanalytical jargon.

A: The hypothesis that he was poisoned is a sort of defence of Muhammad. It means sanctifying him further and absolving him of all sin. He remains the great one, and the others traitors.

H: You're saying that this hypothesis, rather than humanizing Muhammad, further immortalizes him.

A: Absolutely. On the other hand, you could say Muhammad was exploited right to the end of his life.

H: So it's the political aspect that shoots to the fore and not Muhammad's murder as the founder and because he was the founder.

A: He wasn't assassinated as a prophet or Messenger bearing a divine word, but as head of a political organization that was emerging in Arabia at that time. His assassination, if that's what it was, would therefore have had a political impact, not a spiritual one.

H: In *Moses and Monotheism*, Freud writes that the difference between Christians and Jews is that the former admitted the murder whereas the latter denied it, and that anti-Semitism chimes in with this.

A: You don't find that verticality in Islam.

H: In an earlier conversation,[13] you said that emigration from Mecca to Medina didn't really constitute exile. In light of what you're saying now, we could say that there's no more exile in Islam than there is murder.

A: It's the economy and the quest for power that takes precedence in Muslims' relations with Muhammad. Even when it comes to this hypothesis of his assassination, it's an Islamic version of assassination, not Jewish or Christian.

H: It may well be that the fact that Islam was imposed by violence prevented the construction of a true theory about the self and the other, about belief and faith, the invisible as a condition of all sight, an individual's choices and desires, life and death, the world and the things of this world … As conversion happened in a climate of terror and hate, this very likely short-circuited the possibility of thinking through the very meaning of conversion, of belief … Thinking requires distance and the presence of Eros. The only wellspring lies at some remove, in the margins.

A: Absolutely. And this proves yet again that Islam was used and exploited for power in the total absence of a spiritual dimension. Quite obviously, the historic conditions have changed. Yet, the gaze trained on the world, on power and on the things of this world, has remained unchanged. It's still the gaze of the rulers and not of the people.

H: Abū Bakr and Umar, the founders of the first caliphate, were rich and extremely powerful before the advent of Islam, and they got outrageously richer, thanks to their conquests. The real revolution, in the sense of a people rising up against tyranny and demanding justice and equal rights, was the one involving the Zanj and the Qarmatians.[14]

A: There you have the whole complexity of Islam from the start. If Sa'd ibn Ubāda's proposal concerning the division of power had been adopted, Islam may well not have survived. We don't know. What we do know, on the other hand, is that dialogue was banned by Abū Bakr and Umar, and that violence is an essential part of Islam and of its foundation. Saqīfa lives on, since it's the same logic that rules us today. The spirit of Saqīfa continues to reign.

5

The City of God and Entitlement

H: The issue of the law in Islam remains intrinsically linked to the Qur'anic Text, to the *ḥadīth* and the interpretative texts. In the absence of any secularism, the legal system still draws on the texts written in the first years of the foundation. While saying 'No compulsion is there in religion',[1] Islam remains the only religion to follow.

A: And at the same time: 'O Prophet, urge on the believers to fight.'[2] This is what turns Islam into a non-stop assault on a person's human rights, and on his freedom, especially in countries where beliefs and practices are pluralist, like Syria, Lebanon, Egypt, Palestine, Jordan … In those countries, citizens are equal only before their obligations. There is such a contradiction between religion and human rights, in Arab and Muslim countries, that we get the feeling Muslims are against progress and against civil life, as if they were living outside History in complete ignorance of the technological revolutions of this world.

H: And what about this verse, already cited, which makes you bristle: 'I have not created *jinn* and mankind except to serve Me.'[3]

A: Muslims think and live as if man were created for religion and not the other way round. Well, religion was created for man. I don't read that verse as a word of God but as an invention of Muslims.

H: So we're dealing with a grandiose ego and therefore with the narcissistic dimension of Muslim man.

A: This narcissistic dimension is expressed in the name of God. It confirms our sense that the Muslim God is an Arab invention. The Arabs adopted all the already known attributes of the biblical God and beefed up the unsurpassable aspect. They proceeded in similar fashion by creating a human model defined as the most elevated on Earth. And so, whoever believes in this model and applies its imperatives also becomes – in turn – an elevated model on Earth.

H: Whoever follows the best of men becomes the best of men. It's the issue of the ego-ideal.

A: Within this logic of 'he who obeys Muhammad in fact obeys God'. It's as if Muhammad said to believers: 'Your attitude towards me is like my attitude towards God.' Result: a cancellation of the individual faced with Muhammad that persists right up to the present day, when what it's really all about is an individual taking the place of God. You're right to say it involves a narcissism that's human, not divine.

H: That verse cancels out the master–slave dialectic. In Ovid's *Metamorphoses*, faced with the wrath of Jupiter, who wants to wipe out the human race, the gods voice their concern. 'And who would pay their altar dues, whose hand bring incense?' From Ovid to Hegel, via Diderot, there is a master–slave dialectic. The idea even exists in children's literature. We find it, for example, in Saint-Exupéry's *The Little Prince*, where the monarch begs the Little Prince to stay with him, since royalty can't exist without a subject (subjects) to rule.

A: Islam invented a world that's like a sealed egg containing only Muslims. It rejects anything that might remind it of difference. Difference is personified by those it calls infidels. Entering into Islam means shutting yourself away in this egg.

H: An egg is what Freud uses as an example when he talks about primary narcissism. He gives the example of a chick in its shell.

A: That example will do me nicely. We could say Islam appropriated the world, in contempt of man and of the world.

H: This division of the world into Muslims and infidels is very problematic. 'God forgives not that aught should be with Him associated.'[4] According to that logic, God condemns an unbeliever to eternal punishment, even if he's upright, generous and just, whereas He forgives a perverse or unjust or tyrannical believer.

A: And according to that logic, a man of no merit could be considered great through the simple fact of belonging to Islam.

H: In short, He forgives you for stealing, raping, killing innocents, spreading ruin … But not for associating Him with another god. What, in fact, is this human frailty that pictures such a narcissistic God? We need to weigh up the philosophical, theological and social consequences of such a concept of the divine.

A: This means that power can't be shared, that there is just one power. And since power can't be shared, 'blind conformism' (*attaba'iyya*) has to be absolute. Let's sum up: the prophet says nothing on his own, decrees nothing, since he has no opinion about anything, everything comes to him from God. This well-crafted novel reveals itself to be a fabulous construction: in the same way that Muhammad was subject to divine will, so the Muslim has to apply the rule of 'blind conformism'. He doesn't even ask himself the question of how it is that God entrusts such important causes and operations to a person who can't read or write, or how the divine word can be entrusted to common people.

H: Those common people have always been glorified and put on a pedestal in the Muslim world. All you have to do is look at the respect with which people still, to this very day, surround the *fuqahā'*,[5] the imams and anyone either closely or remotely connected to religion.

A: Following the *fuqahā* means that recitation takes the place of reflection and thought, and that the oral tradition triumphs over the written word.

H: That kind of memory has to be questioned. The hagiographers say that when Umar wanted to share the tribute on *ḥafaẓa al-Qur'an*,[6] he had a few problems, because the men, having been involved in wars, had no way of learning the Qur'an. Their knowledge of the Text, as we have said, was very rudimentary.

A: That's only logical. No human being in a context of war or conquests can afford the luxury of learning the Qur'an by heart and passing it on.

H: This other verse – 'He chastises whom He will, and forgives whom He will'[7] – shocks, intellectually and emotionally, as it expresses the law of the arbitrary. Now, arbitrariness is a generator of anxiety and of a desire to submit so as not to anger the Other. I think that's the very test of totalitarianism.

A: Absolutely. You could say that monotheism is an extremely powerful machine, perhaps the best invention you could find for subjugating human beings.

H: 'O believers, shall I direct you to a commerce that shall deliver you from a painful chastisement?'[8] Where you were expecting some expression like 'a good work' or 'a work of charity', the term chosen is 'commerce'. This fits in with what you were saying.

A: The verse continues like this: 'You shall believe in God and His Messenger, and struggle in the way of God.' The link between commerce and combat is clear. Combat on behalf of the religion isn't spontaneous, it doesn't spring from the profound convictions of the believer in his love of God or religion. It's more a matter of a trading operation or paid work. The believer works for a reward and not for some human objective, like making the world a more beautiful place, for example, or making it more open to science, knowledge and progress. Muslims are paid 'soldiers' in a barracks commanded by the Islamic government.

H: The fact that jihad, in this verse, is linked to belief in God and in his prophet, as well as to such remuneration, has serious consequences. We haven't yet taken the time to reflect on the collapsing of the metaphysical into the political, on the impact of these verses on people who are extremely fragile psychologically, or on their hijacking by imams in the service of Wahhabism to spread dangerous ideologies.

A: The consequences are disastrous because, on divine orders, the martyr allows, authorizes and makes licit all that the Muslim desires: *saby*,[9] looting, theft … That said, for a man to help himself according to his heart's desire is a sort of commerce (*tijāra*).

H: '*Saby* and looting', sexuality and cruelty combined. The verse goes on:

> He will forgive you your sins and admit
> you into gardens underneath which
> rivers flow, and to dwelling-places
> goodly in Gardens of Eden; that is
> the mighty triumph.[10]

The gift of your life will be rewarded by paradises where river streams flow, along with honey and wine. That's a sort of divine commerce.

A: Of course. I take your lives and God will award you a prize. Consequently, anyone who doesn't make jihad is banned from this commerce.

H: That binary logic is a logic of exclusion because: 'The true religion with God is Islam.'[11] Added to the other one, this verse can fuel extremism since, for certain people, belief goes hand in hand with martyrdom, which goes hand in hand with trade.

A: It's a religious culture that teaches people permissiveness, crime and the lifting of prohibitions, as well as contempt for the human and for humanity.

H: And no one even dares say that images of gardens with their flowing streams can be seen as the fabrication of an imaginary world that's the opposite of the aridity of Mecca. 'Neither your blood-kindred nor your children shall profit you upon the Day of Resurrection.'[12] The family unit and libidinal bonds find themselves undone in this verse. Which can be understood as a force for social unbonding. Whenever there's a terrorist attack, I find myself again asking this twofold question: how does an individual come to take the life of another individual? And how is it that he doesn't think of the grief he'll be causing that person's closest relations, his family, his brothers and sisters … ?

A: But if you love God, you've got everything. And woe betide the ungodly!

H: Stalinist logic called for the dissolution of the family in aid of the ideology. And on the subject of the ungodly, 'And let not the unbelievers suppose that the indulgence We grant them is better for them; We grant them indulgence only that they may increase in sin; and there awaits them a humbling punishment.'[13] Why such punishment, then, since he's the one who decides who'll be impious? Doesn't he say, precisely: 'God leads astray whomsoever He will, and whomsoever He will He guides.'[14] And: 'No affliction befalls, except it be by the leave of God.'[15] God wrote everything before the human race turned up. Why punish those whom he himself has not accepted into his ranks?

A: And: 'Say to the unbelievers: "You shall be overthrown, and mustered into Gehenna".'[16] This aligns with what we've already mentioned, namely the problem of *naskh*.[17] Either God knows everything, for all eternity, and consequently has no need to abrogate, or there are things he doesn't know. It's a stalemate that shows the experimental side of the Qur'an at the same time.

H: '… then their refuge is Gehenna – an evil cradling!'[18] – and this, for all eternity. Why so much hate? Where is Eros? We can't go on dodging the issue of hatred in what is for Muslims the Text of reference and its impact on the psyche: terror, the logic of exclusion, acting out, incitement to martyrdom …

A: The Arabs fabricated a God who detests the human race. They locked the individual away in a prison. And opposite this prison stands the kingdom of God where everything is allowed, where nothing is prohibited. Muslims can do whatever they like, since their acts are done in the name of God. The only possible deduction is this: if Islam advocates theft, usurping goods, assassinations … it's because the Qur'anic Text is a human text, it was written by human hands.

H: I ask the question again: what is this psyche that is full of such hate?

A: As a matter of fact, commerce, all commerce, is a sort of war. History shows that Muhammad and the caliphs who succeeded him were all, apart from 'Alī, traders who managed to set up a very solid structure and a system in which power was held by a single person only. The caliphs succeeded each other in such a way that each one replaced another one.

H: This whole corpus needs much deeper analysis. And Muslims have a duty to reread their history, their Text and their texts. If the other is an adversary to be exterminated in the name of God, what place is left for the guilt and responsibility of the individual?

A: All the more as the adversary to be exterminated is the one whose wealth I am going to take. Mut'ab ibn Qushayr, one of Mohammad's companions, said of the Battle of Uhug: 'Muhammad promised us the riches of the Kisra.[19] Today, no one can quietly go to the toilet.'[20] Gain and love of gain have generated a climate of total mistrust.

H: A climate of paranoia.

A: The model to be followed promised riches on Earth and in Heaven.

H: This issue of the model so pervaded individuals' lives that people went to see Aïsha to ask her for details about Muhammad's intimate life so as to do the same things he did. Even with sexuality, Muhammad was the model. One way of mixing God up in matters of sex.

A: To the present day, the Muslim is proud of imitating Muhammad, including in the act of marrying a little girl of nine.

H: We should remember this phrase of Freud's, though: 'Neurosis is the negative of perversion.' Which is the same as saying that neurosis represses what bursts out into the open with perversion.

A: Why didn't psychoanalysis put in an appearance in the Arab world?

H: First, psychoanalysis is atheist. It deconstructs, desacralizes, de-idealizes, analyses the human being in depth, isn't daunted by negatives, fantasies or urges … The child is a cannibal, the maternal breast is an erotic breast, the father of the original horde was gobbled up by his sons, religion is a collective neurosis, religious ceremonial recalls the ceremonial of obsessional neurosis … All these examples show the freeing up of psychoanalytical thought in relation to the idea of norms, to ideality and to the sacred. Psychoanalysis speaks of desire, of pleasure, analyses inhibitions and is part and parcel of the freedom of the individual. Psychoanalysis is antinomic to all we've been talking about till now.

A: So, rejection of psychoanalysis in the Arab world taps

into the split in the Muslim Arab man who takes everything that comes from Western science but rejects the principles of thought that have produced that science. Muslims take all technology but reject the intellectual principles that have led to technological progress. This contradiction expresses the spirit of legend that dominates the depiction of life and thought in the Arab world.

H: Psychoanalysis puts magical thinking in the same category as feelings of omnipotence. If it looked closely at our works of so-called hagiography, it would see the fantasy, the excess, the voyeurism, the irrationality of desire, as in Sade, and which, in offering itself up to God's gaze, feels to me like something out of Bataille. This structure has never been analysed. And one of the reasons why psychoanalysis hasn't entered the Arab world, it seems to me, is the fear of exposing these incredibly dark, encysted zones that have never been analysed in a corpus of reference that demonstrates to what extent perversion is the positive of neurosis.

A: Basically, Islam is interpreted and lived as a permissiveness and a perversion. Fifteen centuries have shored up what we've been talking about today and what we're fighting against. The mindset is so pervaded by all the prohibitions on thought and by legends rooted in the social and cultural fabric that it can only reject what we are discussing today. For fifteen centuries a battle has been raging against thought and against human freedom.

H: In those fifteen centuries, though, there have been revolts, like the ones we've already mentioned by the Zanj and the Qarmatians, and also by mystics, philosophers and poets.

A: All those revolts were put down and dispersed by the machinery of power. And it's this power structure that has stopped the Text from ever becoming a subject of study and reflection. Since the individual's submission to God is absolute, man's future is written in advance. He can neither choose nor negotiate.

H: That's a big difference from polytheism, in which the individual negotiated with the gods.

A: The Muslim prefers to refer to what he assumes is the will of God. He doesn't even follow the example of *Iblīs*.[21]

H: In the Qur'an, *Iblīs* converses with God.

A: *Iblīs* is able to choose. In the same way that paradise doesn't triumph over Gehenna (hell), God doesn't triumph over *Iblīs*.

H: They are complementary and necessary to each other.

A: God needs *Iblīs*. *Iblīs* is eternal like he is. Paradise and Gehenna are like God and Satan. Within Islam, known individuals and groups like the Batinites[22] cancelled out the material and physical sense of paradise and hell. They gave them a symbolic and metaphoric meaning.

H: Whether to take everything literally or interpret it metaphorically? The question of interpretation is one of the richest and most complex questions within Islam. It's also the value of reading: how do we read?

A: And above all, what is the value of what is known as Revelation today? Knowledge is an integral part of power. And vice versa. Furthermore, knowledge has to submit to power, because power is divine. We could talk about the identical nature of power and knowledge. Evil is whatever is defined as such by God-the-prophet. Good, likewise. The only path to God is Islam, the only prophet is the prophet of

Islam, the only God is the God of Islam. In its very essence, Islam is power.

H: Al-Fārābī, the founder of political philosophy in the medieval Muslim Arab world, advocated a political philosophy that interlaced the political science of the Ancients, Plato's *Republic* and Aristotle's *Politics*, with religion. He reckoned that religion needed to be interpreted and that philosophy was an indispensable prerequisite for founding the City of Virtue (*al-madīna al-faḍīla*), that religious laws were only necessary for people whose morality was weak, and that virtuous people (who are endowed with the faculty of reason) needed neither fixed practices nor laws.

A: The philosophy of al-Fārābī has no place in Islam as religion and politics.

H: And yet he's just as necessary as Machiavelli saying that man can control his destiny, or as La Boétie reflecting on voluntary servitude. I draw attention to the fact that La Boétie's work has only recently been translated into Arabic, by Moustapha Safouan, and of course it isn't taught, any more than Machiavelli is.

A: Arab governments prefer to go on teaching the tradition rather than making a break with voluntary servitude. Herd-like conformism shows how far man contributes, clings and binds himself to his own enslavement.

H: Today, because we're lacking a Fārābī, an Averroès, a Descartes, a Nietzsche, a La Boétie, a Machiavelli … in the Arab world, conflicts are occurring just as they did in the days of Muhammad. I was struck by an article on the issue of *diya*[23] in Iraq. People who've lost loved ones and family members are demanding *diya*. The individual is still operating under the legal code of the foundation.

A: This *diya* was around before Islam. Islam didn't abolish it: it maintained it.

H: We might quote Nietzsche here: 'Finally, to show the downside of these religions as well as to throw light on their uncanny dangers: there is a high and horrible price to pay when religions do *not* serve as means for breeding and education in the hands of a philosopher, but instead serve themselves and become *sovereign*, when they want to be the ultimate goal instead of a means alongside other means.'[24] The hegemony of a belief is what legitimizes the violence of the political.

A: What's most catastrophic is that the violence only intensifies in Muslims who think that this violence is closest to their faith. The more intensely they believe, the more violent they have to be to get the blessing of a God who gives himself the attributes of vengeance, tyranny and torture. In their imagination, the more victims they make, the bigger their reward will be. And the worst thing is that those who rule in the name of Islam are often ignoramuses.

H: Not a single scientist or intellectual among the men who founded the group, the Muslim Brotherhood, whose motto is 'God is our objective, the prophet our leader, the Qur'an our constitution, jihad our path, martyrdom our greatest hope.' Not a single one of them (Ḥasan al-Bannā, Ḥāfiẓ 'abd al-Hamīd, Aḥmad al-Ḥaṣrī, Fu'ād Ibrāhīm, Abd al-Raḥmān Ḥasballāh, Ishmael Azz) was an intellectual, or even a scholar in the theological sciences.

A: Culturally and intellectually, the Muslim world is poor.

6

Tillage? Woman, the Most Noble of Words[1]

H: All the hagiographies talk about the role of Khadīja in the foundation of Islam.

A: Khadīja's role was decisive in the construction of Islam. Of course, she was assisted by Waraqa ibn Nawfal. That said, her role in the foundation was more than crucial.

H: I recall that Waraqa was a scholar with vast knowledge of the religious corpus of his time, in particular of monotheism. I also recall that he was a Christian convert to the *ḥanīfiyya* religion and that he had a big influence on Muhammad.

A: Waraqa was also surrounded by Nestorians. And the position of the Qur'an on Christianity is a Nestorian position.

H: In the hagiographies, Islam remains tied to Khadīja's name. The future of Islam, they say, depended on her word as she was the one who identified the angel, thereby rescuing Muhammad from anguish and doubt. Her word was decisive. Can she be considered a founding figure?

A: It's very hard to map out a history based on references from that particular time. We can, nevertheless, draw a few conclusions by relying on what has come down to us as narratives about the historic period covering Muhammad's life with Khadīja. That's a period of twenty years. It's a long time.

H: All the narratives agree that Khadīja, who was a trader, gave Muhammad the job of conducting her caravan to Shām and that Muhammad showed great deftness in getting a return on her money. Some hagiographers say she loved him for his *amāna*,[2] other sources say she was seduced by his physical appearance and his eloquence. But we read everywhere that Muhammad was singled out, by Buhaira, as the future prophet of the Arabs.

A: We can deduce, from these narratives, that Khadīja thought about prophecy for a quarter of a century. From her first meeting with Muhammad up to the day he uttered his prophecy. Some narratives also say that Muhammad hesitated when it came to accepting the prophecy, that he was afraid of accepting the idea. Why this hesitation? He's been described as having a weak personality, weak in terms of taking a stand and making decisions.

H: Yet history was to show the reverse.

A: He became more robust after the prophecy. I think Khadīja played an essential role in persuading Muhammad to accept the prophecy. She lit the way for him. Her power was enormous.

H: Can we say that it was she who made Muhammad?

A: Khadīja was not only a great trader or a great capitalist. She was at the head of Qurayshite society. She worked at getting him to accept the idea. She constructed the prophecy with her cousin Waraqa ibn Nawfal and the Nestorians of the day. We need to show the role of the feminine in the prophecy.

H: The role of the feminine or the role of women?

A: Prophetic masculinity is inhabited by prophetic femininity in Muhammad.

H: The hagiographers have drawn her as a complex figure. She's been depicted above all as a very powerful woman, one who was happy to play a maternal role for Muhammad.

A: That fact should be studied in light of the relationship, but it's true we lack historical documents. That said, I see her as the first founder or among the first founders of Islam.

H: In that case, we might venture a question that could be considered blasphemous: was it out of intellectual and/or spiritual conviction, or out of ambition? Was it a call for a sublime Other World, or the desire to rule?

A: Khadīja represented the pragmatic aspect that enabled and prepared the establishment of political power. She was able to pave the way for her husband thanks to her economic power. As well as that, she grasped the full importance of the Revelation as an ideology of power and exploitation of the Revelation as a sort of commerce, trade. We could even say she created both an earthly trade and a heavenly trade. It's very hard now to understand the heavenly world if we disregard the earthly world in which Islam saw the light of day. The goal was to replace Jewish hegemony on the Arabian Peninsula with an Arab hegemony.

H: At that moment, then, we could say that it wasn't the spiritual aspect that motivated her but the desire to conduct herself like an empress, the desire to rule.

A: Absolutely. And as we mentioned earlier several times, the spiritual aspect only made its debut in Islam with Sufism, that is to say two hundred years after the foundation. The language of early Islam was commercial: rivers of milk, rivers of wine, pleasures and tortures …

H: In one narrative, we read: 'The women were by the Ka'ba making offerings to the god Hubal. A Jewish passer-by said: "Anyone wishing to marry a prophet should not delay."' Since Maisara, Khadīja's slave, had told Khadīja about Buhaira's sermon, Khadīja sent her sister to Muhammad to ask for him in marriage.

A: She was no ordinary woman. Even though she was very rich, she rejected the position of a traditional woman and continued, after the deaths of her first two husbands, to engage in commerce. She enjoyed a prestigious position in Meccan society. She was one of the grandes dames of Arabia. Why was she marginalized, and even neglected, after the foundation? I'm amazed that researchers and historians of Islam haven't taken the time to reflect on that question.

H: The hagiographers mention her decisive role, in the beginning, only to then consign her to a secondary place after the foundation. In historical constructions, she was divested of her strength as a woman and of her audacity, only to become nothing more than the mother of her prophet. She was 'everything' to Muhammad.

A: We could say that that was the beginning of a decline in the female condition. The reduction of a woman's role to a diminishing asset to the advantage of masculine domination. The great paradox is that Islam, which was born in the bosom of femininity, grew and developed with emphatic virility. The hagiographers neglected Khadīja so as to push Muhammad further to the front of stage. She's the one who launched him by entrusting him with her trade with Shām. At a certain period, Muhammad was just the commercial face of Khadīja. As much as she was a lady, he started out as just a simple trader. And as I said, faced with his anguish and hesitation, she gave him the reassurance that led to certainty. We could even say that she was his path to certainty.

H: We could also say that Muhammad listened to the woman who could see into his heart.

A: When she says, 'it's an angel', Muhammad greeted her word with conviction. How can the hagiographers have stripped a woman like Khadīja of the presence she deserves when she was the voice that reassured their prophet? Muhammad's relationship with his wife shows that she played a central role in his prophecy. This is something that hasn't really been studied by researchers.

H: Not like that. I read that, before the advent of Islam, the women of Arabia were strong and free. To confine women to a secondary role goes hand in glove with the construction of Islam as a corpus and as a practice. The verses that require the wives of the prophet to veil themselves and require husbands to beat their wives came after Khadīja's death.

A: This leads me to note: she played a decisive role in the advent of Islam, but this presence was covered up, starting with the four caliphs. The Arabs couldn't stand a woman having such a role. That's why she was eclipsed.

H: Apart from material affluence, Khadīja fulfilled a psychological need in Muhammad. How else can we fathom the radical change in Muhammad's behaviour? He was monogamous the whole time he was married to Khadīja, but then just went on making conquest after conquest after she died. Was it because Khadīja was the wife-mother and Muhammad couldn't resign himself to not having a woman who was everything to him? Was possessing every woman he came across a maniacal way of expressing a grief that was unbearable? Or was it the phallic side of Islam that was accentuated by his conquests?

A: Islam legitimized the possession of women. I think it's also about the triumph of the Bedouin Arab mindset, which is all about virility, power.

H: But polyandry existed in Arabia before Islam. Which says a lot about the freedom of women and their right to do what they liked with their bodies.

A: That's true. The importance of women before Islam is borne out by history. There were women prophets, poets, rulers … But with the arrival of Islam, the presence of women on the social and political scene suffers a significant decline. Women were confined to a secondary role.

H: Sajāḥ was a poet, prophet and chief of four tribes in southern Arabia. This means that men accepted a woman's having that status.

A: The decline in the position of women in society can be explained, it seems to me, by two things. So as to shore up Muhammad's place as founder, the hagiographers glossed over Khadīja's presence, promoting Muhammad from a secondary role to the role of sole ruler. The second thing is that the Text itself diminished the importance of women. And yet, we can understand the marginalization of Khadīja in light of what happened to Muhammad himself, after his death.

H: You're saying that the power that downplayed

Muhammad's death also triumphed over Khadīja, once she was dead. In that case, I go back to what I said a moment ago: Muhammad, who was monogamous, suddenly switched to polygamy after the death of his first wife – to the point where he took a little girl of six and consummated the marriage two years later.

A: It may be that Muhammad took Aïsha to benefit from Abū Bakr's power. After Khadīja's death and the death of his uncle Abū Talib, he was alone and weakened. So he needed alliances. Now, Abū Bakr was one of the most important figures in Mecca. The union gave him the power he'd lost. This proves, yet again, the importance of Khadīja. Once she was gone, Muhammad didn't have a base anymore. He had to clutch at something.

H: If we say that his marriage after that to Ḥafṣa, Umar's daughter, followed the logic of alliances, then that means the relationships between men were conducted through the bodies of women and little girls. And since Muhammad is a role model who's meant to be emulated, marriage to young teenage girls and prepubescent girls still exists today. In Yemen, a little girl of ten recently took herself off to see a judge to get a divorce because her husband 'wanted things she didn't want'.

A: First, you have to condemn a society that accepts this fact. Second, how could Muhammad take a little girl, and how can a believer accept that his prophet married a little girl? How could the father hand over his daughter? How could the mother?

H: The hagiographers only talk about Abū Bakr. Very little has been said about the mother. She's mentioned only to say she had trouble giving birth and that it was Khadīja who helped her give birth to Aïsha.

A: The idea that Khadīja helped Aïsha's mother give birth to Aïsha is interesting. It's as if they were saying that by marrying Aïsha, he was marrying Khadīja for the second time.

H: He fulfilled all his fantasies, in that case.

A: Psychoanalytical analysis is called for.

H: We spoke of how Khadīja was able, in the hagiographical writings, to identify the angel. Because the angel fled at the sight of a woman's hair. We said that that particular narrative stacked up from a psychoanalytical point of view but not from a historical point of view. I ask you this: how come an angel who flees from Khadīja's hair looks at little Aïsha in Muhammad's bed without batting an eyelid, and then delivers the Revelation?

A: Muhammad was always consoled by Khadīja whenever he had his attacks. He hid his face in her bosom and she'd console him … It may be that he had the same attitude to Aïsha as Khadīja had to him.

H: Muhammad said: 'Gabriel only visits me when I am with Aïsha.' Literally, 'when I am in Aïsha's bed'. How can the hagiographers have concocted a story about a Revelation that could only take place in the bed a man shared with a little girl?

A: And wasn't Muhammad embarrassed to receive the angel when he was with Aïsha?

H: For me, Aïsha's revolt, which drove her to launch the Battle of the Camel,[3] is a reaction to the harm she'd suffered. Through the Battle of the Camel, they say, she weakened Muhammad's clan and facilitated the Umayyads' access to power. It was her way of taking her revenge on her prophet husband, on the precepts of Islam which demanded that the wife of the prophet not leave his house, and on Khadīja.

A: In politics as well as in everyday life, she was against Muhammad himself and against his desires. She was a rebellious woman. And she remains one of the founders after Muhammad. Khadīja founded an Islam in Muhammad's lifetime, and Aïsha founded one after his death. No Arab or Muslim woman has ever learnt the lesson in audacity and courage they ought to have learned from Aïsha.

H: Her revolt was justified by the damage she'd suffered in her childhood and early adolescence. For it was in Aïsha's room that the angel authorized Muhammad to take Zaynab, the wife of his adopted son, as his fifth wife, with the result that symbolic filiation in Islam was abolished.

A: Isn't that a bit of make-believe that aligns with the make-believe of prophecy?

H: Well then why hasn't this bit of make-believe been deconstructed? Women are presented as debased, possessed, humiliated ... starting with Hājar (Agar), our so-called mother. The Muslim corpus exaggerated the biblical aspect by wondering about her filthiness. Ibn Qutayba and Ibn Kathīr write: 'If she had been filthy, she would not have been *wi'ā'*[4] for Ibrahim.' It's the fact of being *wi'ā'* that saves her from filthiness.

A: We need to deconstruct everything, starting with this question: how is it that Hājar is our mother?

H: That job remains to be done, since only something Muhammad said sets her up as mother. In *Qisas al-'Anbiyā'* by Tha'ālibī[5] we find these words of Muhammad, 'May God take our mother Agar into his mercy', in the form of a rebuke. She is supposed to have rushed to give Ishmael something to drink. If she hadn't hurried, the spring would have been inexhaustible, says Muhammad. She's not even mentioned in the Qur'an. And in the Encyclopaedia of Islam, she pops up in the chapter on Ishmael. Talk about being badly treated!

A: That's an area for you to think about. Women become historically subjugated after the death of Khadīja.

H: The hagiographers wrote or passed on stories without thinking of the consequences that would follow. For example, that fact that, after a military win, Muhammad could immediately take a woman who pleased him and marry her, without going through a third party. In actual fact, that spells the cancellation of marriage as a symbolic institution.

A: It's really important to say these things like this. The prophet no longer needed an intermediary. He gave himself the freedom to do what he liked. It's clear there was a big gap between the personality of Muhammad as prophet representing God on Earth and his behaviour with women. We need to seriously study a corpus that depicts a prophet transgressing ethics and morality. If we want to reflect, one day, on the gap in a *ḥākim*[6] between theory and practice, we'd need to start by going back over our history.

H: Taking a little girl as a wife and allowing yourself the wife of your adopted son didn't even exist in paganism, described as a time of *jāhiliyya.*[7]

A: We read in the hagiographies that when Muhammad saw that one of the Muslims fighting alongside him in his cause had a beautiful wife, he took her from him. This merits a psychological study. What's certain is that he was not known to have had other relationships before Khadīja.

Khadīja was mother and wife rolled into one. And once he'd laid his hands on the wife-mother, anything was allowable, it was a free-for-all. He opened up to all kinds of experiences. The fact of having had Khadīja smoothed the way for him to do what he liked.

H: We are steeped in this culture so we don't have the necessary distance to question the cultural factors. Why four wives? Why not five or three or two? I found a *ḥadīth* that says: 'I am the son of four mothers.' Does that come down to saying: 'I authorize the same number of mothers I've had'? At the same time, I go beyond that number in my capacity as prophet.

A: It's a personality created by the Revelation itself. In fact, there needs to be a study done analysing the evolution of Muhammad's personality as he moves through the Revelation. How do the verses paint the prophet's personality?

H: It's that model that constitutes the ego-ideal for Muslims.

A: Any doubt, any questioning, any query, threatens to bring the role model crashing down. Muslims need a man who's perfect.

H: Yet, the little nine-year-old girl is there to remind us that the model needs to be questioned.

A: It's God who tells him to take her. And so, it becomes legitimate. People need to listen carefully to what Muhammad says about women. What did he say about Khadīja? Not a lot.

H: When Aïsha poured scorn on her, saying she was just an old woman, Muhammad replied: 'She took me in when

I was an orphan, she protected me when others rejected me and she gave me children.' You can almost hear Sophocles' *Oedipus Rex*.

A: Indeed.

H: In the best-known version, Muhammad lost his father when he was still in his mother's womb, and she died when he was six. Today we'd say: the imagination fabricated the fantasy image of a little infanticide boy greedy for a mother's breast. The four mothers would be the answer to the craving of this child orphan. A craving that makes him single out Faṭima as the mother of his father. As for Khadīja, she was more of a mother to Muhammad than she was to her own children.

A: They all died except for Faṭima, who was one of the living dead.

H: In the hagiographical writings, she went back to being a virgin again after every act of intercourse with 'Alī. Which is a way of saying that she remained a virgin for the father. And Muhammad said of his grandchildren: 'All children belong to their father, except Faṭima's children, who are my children.'

A: His love for Faṭima was a sort of love for his mother. But why didn't Muslim women follow Aïsha's example?

H: Some women broke with the traditional status of women in Arabia. Sukayna, Muhammad's great-granddaughter, was a poet even though the Qur'an prohibits poetry.

A: She was on her own, unfortunately. But it may well be that there were women whose names and stories haven't come down to us.

H: When I was translating *Diwan de la poésie arabe classique*[8] with you, I discovered female poets who spoke freely of their desire and their pleasure. Such as A'rabiyya, who groaned out loud with pleasure, twice a day: 'She groans at nightfall and groans again when dawn sparkles. Without those two groans, she'd go mad.'[9] But the historians stripped these women of their names and of any biographical note, whereas they kept the names of melancholy or platonic poetesses. As soon as a woman talks about her body or her flesh, censorship battens down on her.

A: There were women heretics and subversives. For instance, al-Arji said: 'What would Minan and its pilgrims be if she didn't go there?'[10]

H: That's a man speaking, not a woman. And so it doesn't pose a problem.

A: He's blaspheming. Because the pilgrimage became a place for lovers. In the absence of the beloved woman, Mecca was of no interest. The example of Sukayna has remained a one-off.

H: We might remember Rābi'a, the woman from the second century Hijra Era, who, five hundred years before Theresa of Avila, transformed the intellectual and religious scene into an erotic and amorous one, thereby shattering all existing idols and dogmas. 'What do I care about some Ka'ba?' she said. 'I want the God of the Ka'ba.'

A: That's one single example.

H: Aïsha was also an example. And Khadīja is an example, too.

A: Unlike the pre-Islamic era, when women were truly free, with the Muslim foundation, these liberated women constitute rare, isolated cases. Religious faith has always been anti-women. On top of that, if a woman isn't independent financially, she can't be free to manage her life the way she'd like. Khadīja's strength also stemmed from her financial independence, not to say her immense wealth.

H: I recall that Khadīja managed the fortune she made as a merchant but that after her death, heaven demanded that Muhammad's wives not leave their homes.[11]

A: As I said, Islam didn't set women free, quite the opposite. It straitjacketed them with a whole raft of precepts and rules. Happily, there were women who rebelled. But in general, Arab or Muslim women let themselves be broken in. They turned their backs on this extraordinary presence, the presence of Khadīja or Aïsha.

H: You mean that it was the counter-example that prevailed?

A: Arab women have extraordinary role models, like Sajāḥ. But such examples haven't had the influence they should have had on Muslim women.

H: How can a woman break free when divine words remind her constantly that she is nothing but 'a tillage' that a man can plough however he likes, whenever he likes,[12] and when heaven requires a man to beat her?[13] Those verses, along with the *ḥadīth* that says women are 'devoid of faith and spirit' were taught to us at school, and school was never secular. When we were little girls and boys, we were so stuffed full of this thinking on the inequality of rights that equality seemed aberrant to us.

A: But women can change that verse ('a tillage for you') to their own advantage. There is in actual fact enormous regression. But there is also a kind of fatalism and acceptance of reality on the part of women. Khadīja, Aïsha, Sajāḥ were extraordinary women. But Arab women are like Faṭima.

H: If the individual's ego is crushed, how can a woman stage a revolution? We're dealing with an anthropological context and cultural, educational and social formatting that require superhuman strength for you to overcome your anxieties and sense of guilt. You need a lot of courage to break with the initial libidinal objects, which are internalized role models. Aïsha, like Sajāḥ, had support.

A: They had support. And yet, Aïsha was politically exploited by 'Alī's enemies.

H: She was extremely audacious when she told Muhammad that God was in a hurry to satisfy his desires. She also said to him, concerning the Jews: 'Stop imitating them. Even if you do everything the way they do, they will never believe in you.'

A: I'm sorry Arab women don't really understand how revolutionary those trail-blazing women were. They haven't understood those three women. Faṭima was the exact opposite of Khadīja, Aïsha and Sajāḥ. Yet, it's this model, crushed and mute, that's been adopted by Muslim and Arab women. This, of course, pleases men.

H: Given the privileges the Qur'an grants them, men prefer to keep their dominant role. When the Taliban seized Kabul, they drew up a charter based directly on the Qur'an. They took up the verse that bans women from leaving their houses. Not leaving their houses anymore means they can no longer go to school, the place where emancipation is fostered.

A: Nevertheless, attitudes are changing. Women are, of course, persecuted. But they're starting to speak out and this must continue.

H: Freedom of thought goes hand in glove with sexual freedom. Men's sexual pleasure is not condemned. On the contrary, you only have to look at the imaginary realm of *janna*.[14] You remind us, in *Commencement du corps, fin de l'océan*,[15] of this idea, which is found everywhere in the Muslim theological corpus:

> A man asked the meaning of the verse:
> 'This is what you were promised for the
> Day of Reckoning;
> this is our provision, unto which
> there is no end.'[16]
> The reply was, 'the deflowering of virgins'.[17]

The seventy women God grants a man in paradise are depicted as being all the same, faceless, nameless, without affect or thought … This is actually what we now call the sex-doll fantasy.

A: We're dealing with a loveless sexual imagination. There can be no sexual pleasure for a woman, except within marriage.

H: Otherwise, she's likely to be subject to a so-called honour killing. Over 90 per cent of feminicides in the world occur in Muslim countries.

A: That's dreadful. Historically, in the Arab world, the only woman who was granted permission to live in the world of pleasure was a *jāriya*, a slave who was both a musician and a dancer. But women can live out their desires and pleasures secretly. 'I give my kiss to whoever wants it', said Wallāda.[18]

Women gave themselves to whoever wanted them, but in secret.

H: We want to live out in the open.

A: There is intense contempt in Islam for the female sex, because Islam emerged through conquests and emerged *as* conquest. Conquest gave Muslims total legitimacy. When a Muslim enters a city, it becomes his. He can destroy it, loot it, take its women. That being the case, the position of women in all three religions is the same. A girl doesn't have the same status as a boy. The Bible wasn't particularly soft on women, either.

H: That's true. Yet, male domination is really way over-the-top in Islam. Bilqīs, for instance …

A: The Text doesn't mention Bilqīs.

H: No woman is named in the Qur'an except Mary. In the archaeology of knowledge, we're forced to look in the Old Testament for what constitutes the history of the women who appear in the Qur'an.

A: That is indeed a question. Why aren't women named in the Qur'an? Getting back to Bilqīs, she asked Solomon what colour God was.

H: That's magnificent! She was a poet. In the Book of Kings, she comes along to test Solomon with riddles. Afterwards, she goes back to her own country, having exchanged gifts with Solomon. Well, in the Qur'anic version, Solomon wants to disgrace her and grab her throne. Where the Bible mentions the meeting of a king and a queen, Islam reveals itself to be much more aggressive towards the woman.

A: This shows a real distortion. In actual fact, a woman is a form of property in all three monotheistic religions. She is not raised to the rank of dignified human being. In Judaism, man thanks God for not making him a woman; in Christianity, the fact of conceiving a pregnancy without sin says a lot about the cancellation of woman. And in Islam, woman was not created in the image of God.

H: Whence the greatness of mysticism: 'He created man in his own image. And he created Eve in her own image [*'alā ṣūratihā*]', writes Ibn 'Arabī. But getting back to theology, Islam put in place a legal instrument that allows heaven to annul the marriage of a woman when she becomes a captive. IS has taken up the annulment of the symbolic dimension.

A: A man can even undo symbolic filiation for his own pleasure, as in the story of Zaynab. The story of Zaynab should not be forgotten: 'So when Zayd had accomplished what he would of her, then We gave her in marriage to thee.'[19] Can a god himself interfere in the amorous desire of his prophet? How come God gets mixed up in that?

H: 'It is their desires that human beings call Aphrodite', said Hecuba. In that verse, we see clearly how the woman is used as an object, passed between men. When the first man is finished, the other one takes her. Such thinking can't fail to shock.

A: Objectively, Aïsha is right. Because man was given the possibility to intervene in what became known as Revelation. All this makes it possible for the enemies of Islam to have doubts about the Revelation.

H: The enemies of Islam or those who dare to think. The issue of women in Islam speaks for itself.

A: Islam categorically denies women freedom and anything that touches on their bodies or their desires. A woman is not in control of her body or her fate. And from the moment Islam opposes women's subjectivity, that's a cancellation of love. The relationship between a man and a woman is simply presented by Islam as a relationship of coupling for the purpose of breeding.

H: No religion has ever insisted as much on the man's pleasure. You said in an interview you did for *Transfuge* that the Arab man sees a woman as just a sex organ.

A: There is no place in Islam for love as *huyām*.[20] We could say that in Islam a woman loves only when she doesn't desire the body of the other. Only when she becomes a simple pillow in the conjugal bed or a simple blanket. Islam forgets the priority of love. It imprisons women within the confines of the *shar*ʿ. Even though the experience of love in an individual's life is the most profound experience there is, the most vulnerable, since it's full of the unpredictable and the unknown. Hence its richness, as well. It's the experience of love that gives a human being the certainty that he or she is alive and is able to face the banality of the cosmos.

H: 'No love story in the world can take the place of love', writes Marguerite Duras. If we take the Egyptian films of the 1950s and 1960s, we see women dressing up sexily, dancing, drinking whisky ... But a woman still had to hang on to her virginity. On the one hand, she could present herself as totally modern; on the other, the religious backdrop remained safely intact. It's true that women are starting to throw off the yoke of tradition, but social resistance has been mobilized in a big way these last few years.

A: In actual fact, the uprisings of Arab women throughout different periods in time haven't really taken a legal turn or been institutionalized and, as a result, they haven't been able to spread through the social fabric. The rebellion of women has remained limited and personal. We could even say that the position of women is going backwards.

H: Not only do honour killings still happen in Europe, but their number is increasing.

A: Look at the case of Turkey. After a century of secularism, women are again wearing the veil.

H: These honour killings have led me to look more closely at sociological writings. Work has produced a shift in the position of women. Well, honour killings show us that the laws of capitalism have not really liberated women; a woman can go out to work, bring home money, participate in economic life and be independent financially, but she still has to submit to the rules of chastity. Otherwise, she loses her life or is threatened with losing her life.

A: It's terrible! And it's shameful! The fault lies squarely with Arab Muslim men. It's an outrageously extreme form of the cancellation of the human being. A woman is destined for consumer pleasure and nothing more.

H: The legal system is still based on *Ṣaḥīḥ Muslim*. In the chapter on adultery, Muslim and Bukhārī, our two authorities, tell the story of how a woman confesses to Muhammad that she's had an illicit relationship and is pregnant. Muhammad asks her to come back and see him after she's had the baby and breastfed it. When she comes back, he takes the infant and condemns the woman to being stoned. The man didn't come into it.

A: That's barbaric. The woman is turned into an object in a text that divides the world into licit and illicit. The woman is accused and condemned *a priori*. And from the moment adultery is a possibility, the punishment is there. Well before the act. Now, being means being loved and not being religious. 'I have not created jinn and mankind except to serve Me.' He didn't say: 'I created them to love one another.' Love is connection with the other, it's nobler in its essence than religion. Religion remains an idea. Love is a body.

H: Love can also be an idea!

A: I mean that love doesn't make itself known through an idea, but religion certainly does. Love is basically a body. The magnitude of love can't be reduced to sex. The other – the lover, male or female – opens that perspective to me. He tells me who I really am. He gives me what is deepest in me, what lies in the depths of my soul and my being. Islam, which is concerned solely with rites and precepts, absolutely doesn't come anywhere near the essence of the human being. Quite the opposite, it imprisons him, paralyses him. Islam means limit and end. Love is non-limit and non-end.

H: Love is opening up. An opening up that is problematic in an excessively phallic culture. The fact that a woman can open up causes anxiety in a man.

A: We haven't given enough thought to the impact of the verse that says, *Inkaḥū* (take carnally). There is an unthought realm in Islam. Islam insists on the trivial, vulgar, animal aspect. Sufism, philosophy and poetry are revolts against this animality which imprisons man in such a reductive vision, which, in turn, imprisons the human within the walls of the *shar*ʿ. With its rules and precepts, the *shar*ʿ takes us away from spirituality, which, all things considered, is a personal matter.

H: I link that unthought realm with a sexuality coming to grips with violence. The excess of the sexual exceeds the capacities of the ego. Muslims tinker with what they call modernity and postmodernity. But we have a culture that's far too imbued with religion. Our everyday language (*'inshallāh, bismillāh*[21]...) shows how anchored religion is in our lives.

A: Exactly. The doctrinaire dimension pervades our culture. Hence the need to separate the religious world from the political-cultural world.

H: When I was a young researcher and used to give lectures in Arab countries, certain colleagues would be keener to contradict me than converse with me. I remember that, at a psychoanalysis conference in Fez, I said that the first mark – for Ibn 'Arabī – was a sexual mark, since it stems from the relationship between a calamus and a tablet, and an Algerian male colleague said to the room: 'Don't listen to her.' Yet he's a psychoanalyst and psychoanalysis, by definition, talks about sexuality!

A: I remember I stopped my review *Mawāqif* because of the issue of women. Not one writer, not one lawyer, agreed to talk openly about the issue of women in Islam and the fraught problem of that legacy ...

H: This problem should not just go on forever. Meister Eckardt had something to say against dogma: 'Woman remains the noblest word that can be attributed to the soul, nobler than virgin.'

A: Once again, there's the whole difference between religious speech and poetic speech. Woman! The mystery of the world.

7

'Love's Capital Is Not to Have Any'

H: 'Though I speak with the tongues of men and of angels, and have not charity, I am become as sounding brass, or a tinkling cymbal. And though I have the gift of prophecy, and understand all mysteries, and all knowledge; and though I have all faith, so that I could remove mountains, and I have not charity, I am nothing … And now abideth faith, hope, charity, these three; but the greatest of these is charity.'[1] There's nothing like that in the Qur'an.

A: The word 'love' doesn't feature in the Qur'an or in the *ḥadīth*. What we find, on the other hand, is 'coupling', 'marriage', 'pregnancy', 'menses' … In Islam, the relationship between a man and a woman is reduced to 'business' for the satisfaction of desire or for begetting children. Islam reduces man, at the heart of this business, to two things: worship of God in the name of the hereafter and worship of instincts in the name of the here below. The saying goes, furthermore: 'Work for the hereafter as if you were going to die tomorrow, and for the here on Earth as if you were going to live forever.' Man turns into something like a machine for producing worship, on the one hand, and happiness, on the other.

H: There's a huge gap between the Qur'anic Text and the books of exegesis of the mystical text and this has the merit of subverting the religious scene.

A: Sufism is a volcanic movement that erupted within Islam. It rejected the *shar'* and the rites while keeping Islam as a subject for interpretative thinking. It stands opposed to what's known as Islamic culture.

H: From the Ancients to the Moderns, man has paid homage to the god Eros. This dimension – to love and be loved – is missing in the Qur'anic Text. The only verse that mentions love is in line with the precepts: 'God will assuredly bring a people He loves, and who love Him.'[2] In fact, in Ṭabarī's commentary, this is all about God's revenge on those who choose a religion other than Islam, by bringing in, in their place, men who love him – that is, who respect the Muslim precepts. They will be loved. And that will be their gratification.

A: In general, Sufism is an invention of another Islam and a revolution within Islam, a spiritual explosion. And the love in this verse has nothing to do with the relationship between a man and a woman. We might even say it's a real earthquake.

H: Is it a different way of thinking or a different Islam?

A: Even though they broke away from orthodox Islam, as it was practised by Muhammad and as it is advocated by the *fuqahā'*,[3] the Sufis stayed in the Islam camp for exclusively political reasons. They created an Islam different from the one they were born into by changing the very idea of God. In Islam, God is presented as an abstract power who rules the world and transcends all things, but the Sufis championed an immanent god, a human god in a way.

H: We can detect the influence of Christianity on mystical thinking.

A: The base on which orthodox Islam rests was rocked. Man can be a god. And vice versa. So the Sufis gave existence back its unity. From that point on it's physical and metaphysical at the same time. You can't separate man from existence, or existence from God. The Sufis also overturned the notion of identity. In Islam identity is a sort of inheritance. You inherit an identity the same way you inherit a house. Well, in Sufism, identity is a constant creation.

H: An ongoing identity, one that's constructed, as in this verse of Rilke's: 'We are born somewhere and we build our own beginnings inside us, little by little.'

A: Exactly. In the same way that we can say that man creates his own work or thought, we say he creates his own identity. This thinking creates a different relationship to the other. The world then ceases to be split into believers and unbelievers and becomes a world devoted to the quest for knowledge. And so the other becomes a place where the self who cannot be without the other opens up.

H: The whole issue of otherness lies there.

A: And it's a major revolution in relation to traditional thought.

H: Listening to you talk about knowledge, this phrase of Al-Nifarī's springs to mind: 'Fixed knowledge is fixed ignorance.'[4]

A: Hence the necessity of the other. In order to know himself, the individual must go through the other. This opening up is a movement towards the future. The other then becomes a component element of the self.

H: The same as with love. For in order to love, man must go through the other. The other is intermediate and constitutive.

A: The Sufis have always advocated thinking about otherness, which, as we've said, is an opening up. The world doesn't derive from the past, but from the future. The world is not the past, it's a world to come.

H: Ibn 'Arabī said: '*Wa lā tazālu kun! Wa lā yazālu al-takwīn*' ('The "Be!" is constant. And so creation is recurrent'). That's the law of perpetual transformation.

A: 'You can't cross the same river twice.' The world is a continuous and endless opening, not a reminiscence or a recorded memory.

H: In Greek mythology, the human/divine split is very subtle. The divine converts into the human. And a human can be admitted to Olympus. In mysticism, we find elements of both Christianity and Hellenist thought. Mysticism is a river that remains open to other rivers, and so never ceases to be renewed. Thought embraces method.

A: And just as the Sufis transformed the meaning of the relationship to the other, they also changed the meaning of femininity. Femininity became the matrix of the world. That's how we can make sense of '*kullu makān lā yu'annath lā yu 'awal 'alayh*'.[5] Femininity became the essential basis for existence. If there is a relationship between God and man, that relationship necessarily goes through the feminine.

H: When Ibn 'Arabī speaks about Niẓām, the young woman who was his muse and whom Henry Corbin compares to Beatrice, it's to define her as the creative wellspring in every one of us. Writing in the twelfth century, he specifies that 'humanity is not virility'. And when he speaks of 'the femininity [that] moves through the world', far from this amounting to essentialism, it points to the feminine in each and every one of us.

A: On top of that, the Sufis created a different style and a different language in order to express their ideas. While religion killed language, Sufism opened up the possibilities of language to infinity.

H: It's no longer a case of 'who is speaking?' but of 'where are they speaking from?', as Michel de Certeau put it. The 'I' expresses absence.

A: The way they created another form of writing, the Sufis put me in mind of the Surrealists, who were trying to free themselves from rationalist thought. In Sufi thought, the individual becomes a pure light moving through the world. And existence thereby becomes a kind of melting into the world or a kind of symbiosis with the world. It's in this kind of fusion that writing happens.

H: When we look at sculptures from Mesopotamia or Egypt, we can see how thoroughly those civilizations were immersed in writing and animated by a love of writing. The winged horse of Assyria, which was to provide the figure of Al-Burāq[6] in the Muslim imagination, is covered in writing. It is a written body. The Ancients didn't separate the being from the drawn line.

A: My collages are a sort of extension of that world.

H: Where the Qur'an says, '... it is a glorious Qur'an, in a guarded tablet',[7] Ibn 'Arabī, in his subversiveness, addresses man, saying: 'You are the written text and the leaf that receives the writing.' The Mesopotamians show us this in a quite overwhelming way. There is no being without the writing that's in him and that fills him. We see this in your collages, which speak wonderfully of the plurality of places and times.

A: Saying that it cancelled out all that came before it, Islam turned the world into a tunnel. Worse. This tunnel is the only one in existence. Or a sort of citadel cut off from the world, but imposing its visions and ruling the world. Whereas the world is a horizon that stretches to infinity.

H: In championing Eros because it's inhabited by him, mysticism abounds in themes that stretch to infinity like 'a shoreless ocean'.[8]

A: Since femininity is the world's starting point, love too is the world's fundamental principle. Man can't *be* unless he is love. The world is a relationship between a beloved and his lover. The world is passionate love.

H: 'Aṭṭār, Rūmī, Ḥallāj, Ibn 'Arabī, Rābi'a, Al-Nifarī, Suhrawardī … have all sung of love. They may each have sung of love in their own way, but they all say as one that the god Eros is the driving force of creation and that the world only exists thanks to love.

A: The world is a whole set of relationships. And the best of them – and so, the most elevated – is the relationship between masculine and feminine. We need to create the world in the image of that elevation.

H: The first mark made in the world is the fruit of the loving relationship between the calamus and the tablet.[9] The upright calamus comes down on the tablet to put its mark on it. As for the tablet, it offers itself lovingly. And that's how the line is born, a line that is by definition sexual.

A: And just as the calamus is an erotic symbol, so too is the ink.

H: A moment ago you brought up the process of unveiling as an experience among Surrealists and mystics. That's an unheard-of disruption of the religious orthodoxy, because vision (of the divine) then becomes possible. Here I pay tribute to Rābiʿa, who paved the way for the mystics by talking about love as a path to unveiling. 'May Your veils fall and may I see You.'

A: Running counter to rigorist traditionalist Islam, Sufism extols the virtues of unveiling, thereby signifying that the world's secrets are infinite. Which is one way of saying that the world is infinite, and so is man, and every bit as much.

H: That's where the great modernity of mystical thought lies. Saying 'until the veils fall and I see You', Rābiʿa, as a subversive woman, fosters meditation on the issue of the ban on representation, and on the image and the veil in relation to otherness.

A: As I said, the Sufis gave Islam a different direction and created a different horizon for it. In traditionalist Islam, all is known and all questions have a God-given answer. Whereas in Sufism there is no knowledge without experience. The ready answer is condemned since it represents a cancellation of knowledge. And so, we can say that what's called knowledge in Islam is in fact a veil thrown over knowledge. In Sufism, knowledge is a step towards an unknown and a perpetual unveiling of the infinity of the world and of man – who is a microcosm of the world.

H: Contrary to Ibn al-Fāriḍ, speaking about the fall of the veil, Ibn 'Arabī later said that the veil never falls, that 'the word is a veil' since it hides the nakedness of the thing. Mysticism is shatteringly modern.

A: Indeed. Sufism questions and invites us to think about all that is unknown in the world. Just as God exists beyond man's grasp, so the world exists, not in the known, in what happens, but in what is to come, and the world's greatness lies in the unknown and in this relationship to the unknown. In that sense, Sufism appears as an attack on all the traditional monotheistic religions and constitutes an extremely important revolution in the realm of thought. Sadly, it was fought and obliterated by the institutions of political and religious power.

H: I want to express the Absolute. But I can only talk in general terms. Ḥallāj is an example of this gap between the desire for the Absolute and the quest for a language that can express that Absolute. The issue of language is also central to mysticism.

A: I haven't expressed anything of what I wanted to say. I struggle as hard as I can in order to voice this unknown thing that haunts me. But it remains ahead of me, unattainable, elusive.

H: Al-Nifarī said: 'The more vision expands, the more expression shrinks.' As for Ibn 'Arabī, he wrote: 'Vision and words cannot exist at the same time.' We can't understand mystical thought and grasp its modernity unless we're familiar with the humanities.

A: The image that springs to mind if I want to compare Al-Nifarī to Ibn 'Arabī is that of a beautiful grotto that has no equal in a mountain that has no equal. As for Ḥallāj, he's the one who shouted his transgression of the religious code loud and clear out of love and out of passion.

H: If Iblīs, the fallen angel, refused to bow before Adam, Ḥallāj said, that's because he couldn't change the object of his love. Faced with the disobedience of Iblīs, God said:

'I will torture you for all eternity.'
'You will not look at me.'
'Yes, I will!' God answers.
'Then, Your gaze will lift me above the torture. Do with me what You will.'

A: He shut him up. Actually, Iblīs is the only one God does talk to. Because he is his other face. Iblīs never leaves God's mind since, without him, the word of God loses its meaning and its point.

H: For Ḥallāj, Iblīs is the one who damns himself out of love.

A: Iblīs is the question. God is the answer. The question is always bigger than the answer. Seeing only the answer, completely splitting the two sides of the same question, the Muslim is the most ignorant of human beings.

H: Mysticism opens up intellectual horizons by maintaining the question. 'Whoever knows his soul knows his Lord', Ibn 'Arabī wrote. 'Well, one cannot know himself and consequently cannot know his Lord.' That's our relationship to the unknown.

A: Hence the battle traditionalist Islam has waged against Sufism.

H: That battle is not just a thing of the past. Ibn Taymiyya is not the only one to have battled against Ibn 'Arabī's thinking. Al-Azhar opposed the reissue of *Futūḥāt al-makkiyya*.[10]

A: Knowing through the intellect and reasoning is always limited. Hence the importance of the *khayāl*[11] in Ibn 'Arabī's œuvre, which is a sort of exceeding of the limits. Imagination, if you like, is a form of knowing as unveiling or intuition.

H: Hence the extremely beautiful title of Henry Corbin's book, *Creative Imagination in the Sufism of Ibn 'Arabī.*

A: If materiality stops man from being transformed into light, imagination goes beyond that particular limit, knowing that light is always veiled or always exists behind a veil. Even if you tear off the veils, other veils appear. For the light the veils hide is higher and deeper.

H: You're closer to Ibn 'Arabī than to Al-Anṣārī or Ibn al-Fāriḍ. Commenting on the passage in the Qur'an – where Moses fainted when God unveiled himself on the mountain – Ibn 'Arabī wrote that God unveiled himself through his name An-Nūr,[12] but that this name was a veil over other names.

A: Absolutely. This means that the imagination can't tolerate repetition. In that, it's like love. All that is great loathes repetition. An individual can carry out the same action, but in a way that's different and new each time. No repetition, but an endless creative gesture. Sexuality proceeds in the same way. Just as you can't cross the same river twice, you can't make love the same way twice. Sexuality is a sort of embodiment of discovery. Basically, mysticism is eroticism on a cosmic scale. Man loves trees, fire … Sufism seeks to establish love relationships with the things of this world.

H: Ibn 'Arabī is the most Heraclitean of mystics. 'God never shows himself twice', he wrote. And '*Wa lā tazālu kun! Wa lā yazālu al-takwīn*' ('The "Be!" is constant. And so creation is recurrent'). Just as the spirit of the word is constant, so too is creation.

A: That's why Ibn 'Arabī was rejected by the people of the dogma. Reading him poses a problem. How do we read his work? How do we interpret it? How do we grasp it? In general, Muslims can't read. Ibn 'Arabī is a bomb exploding in the Arab language, in Arab life and in Arab thought. This bomb doesn't obey any order. And that's its greatness.

H: When we read *Futūḥāt*[13] we realize that there is no structural unity. The Text is astructural. *Akbarian*[14] writing is deconstructive writing and I hereby gleefully adopt your expression: 'It's a bomb exploding.'

A: Studies of Ibn 'Arabī that have been done within the framework of Muslim monotheism have veiled his vision and erased his greatness.

H: When he writes at the very beginning of *Futūḥāt*, 'Glory be to Him who created the world from nothing and annihilated that nothing', we're moving in the direction of Hegel or Lacan. Or this statement: 'There is a name we leave and a name we go to and, in-between, the *huwa*.'[15] Benveniste talks about the need for the absent for the structure of language to be able to hold together. That's a very modern thought.

A: People need to rediscover this great thinker outside the framework of Muslim dogma, and of Orientalism and, therefore, of the Western understanding of Ibn 'Arabī.

H: As a thinker of movement, he smashes dogma. I will never forget these lines from *Turjumān al-Ashwāq*:[16]

My heart has become a receptacle of all forms
A pasture for gazelles
And abbey for monks
Temple for idols
And Ka'ba for pilgrims
Tablet of the Torah
And leaves of the Qur'an
The religion of love is the one I profess
Wherever its mounts take themselves
Love is my only faith and my only religion.

A: Those are magnificent lines that say just how far above all the limits drawn by dogmas man is, how he is haunted and inhabited by another world. The monotheisms, particularly the Jewish and Muslim monotheisms, are closed dogmatic forms. Sufism is above all that.

H: The Aleppo theologians protested strongly against Ibn 'Arabī's *Turjumān al-Ashwāq* even though it champions love. In mysticism, unlike in orthodox religion, there is no place for hate. And if there is a negative affect, it is totally sublimated.

A: The Sufist is full of love. But if he were asked to define love, he'd answer that it's only accessible through taste, that it can't be defined in itself. To know it, you have to taste it. But the taste doesn't staunch the thirst. *That* is never quenched.

H: But he also says: 'Drink as much as you like.' For only 'he who is not in love sees his own reflection in the water' (Rūmī). That's the whole difference with Narcissus.

A: As I've already written: love is always in motion and in endless transformation. The lover and the loved are two absent beings. And in union, love is in relationship with a being whose existence never ceases to begin again as if he were longing to find himself in the absent Beloved. If he can't accept division, that's because your heart can't split in two. Since we've raised the issue of imagination, I'd say that imagination is the presence in which the lover loves the image of the loved. In fact, he loves only what he has shaped. What Ibn 'Arabī calls the love of love. As for man's love of God, it begins when he listens to his words.

H: 'He was the first speaker and I was the first listener' (Ibn 'Arabī). Otherness already resides in the voice.

A: It means listening to the mysteries.

H: The mystery of all the things of this world, then.

A: Of course. This ability to listen is what makes existence happen. Sufism can't encompass violence or hate in its thinking, or war and all the cruelty and barbarity that go with it. It means retreat. The negative affect, as you call it, consists in rejecting a world that's too bogged down in materialism and ignorance, in the classical sense of those terms.

H: Such mystical thinking is immensely grand. And you say we need to be familiar with it not just for itself, but also to read Rimbaud.

A: Exactly. Unlike Baudelaire or Mallarmé, Rimbaud had no ties to Western culture. He was drawn to another civilization, which he sought to examine by feel, by touch, and which he tried to get close to through Islam. Rimbaud was very drawn to the unknown side of the Orient.

H: So were others at that time: Nerval, Lamartine, Delacroix …

A: Of course. And still others, like Paul Klee, Nietzsche, Goethe … Except Rimbaud's greatness lies in his revolt against the West. And so, we need to read him within the framework of an Oriental mysticism. All his poetry is full of criticism of the West, and the quest for another world, the Orient.

H: Is that why you call him a Sufi?

A: Naturally, Western intellectuals are reluctant to accept this view of things. In their eyes, Rimbaud remains a Westerner. Whereas he was, like the Sufis, filled with a profound passion for mystery. A mystery he sought to penetrate by reading the Qur'an or travelling to Yemen and far away from the West, more generally.

H: It's true that this part of Rimbaud's life and thought isn't all that well known in France. People focus a lot more on that '*Je* est un autre' ('*I* is another').

A: If we reflect on Ovid's idea that the first mirror was water, this means nature is the first mirror, not industry. The manufactured mirror makes no sense.

H: When we talk about mirrors, of course we go back to Plato's *Alcibiades*, where the other is defined as a mirror. It's not about the manufactured element. It's about the other who reflects my own wholeness back to me.

A: The mirror doesn't only reflect a person's image. Through the image, it reflects the essence of the human being.

H: Which essence remains unknown, is never unveiled. Loss is part and parcel of the mirror. 'Aṭṭār[17] said: 'Who has seen his own face? No one can see their face.'

A: Of course not, since the mirror is a reminder, not knowledge.

H: What depresses me is the way people trying to escape from psychological anxiety are turning to what's known as spirituality, resorting to the mystics as a cure. And in the disarray that radicalization has given rise to, people refer to Sufism to whitewash Islam of any stain of violence, and they do so in complete denial of what gives mysticism its vigour: its heretical stance, its thinking on femininity, the image, the metapsychology of breath, the experimental use of language, the relationship to the Other and to the other … Ibn 'Arabī, for instance, becomes a simple sheik. The force of his thinking is obscured or misrepresented or annulled.

A: Worse than that. Islam is a dogmatic structure. Closed, before the door of knowledge, but also completely opposed to knowledge.

H: I should add that in the 1970s and '80s, people talked about the influence of Christianity on the birth of Sufism. These days, Ibn 'Arabī, in the Andalusia of Ibn Ṭufayl and Maimonides, the contemporary of Averroès, is presented as a sheik theologian who knew nothing about the Greeks but wrote under divine inspiration. He's been taken over by the orthodoxy he challenged and which is trying to tame his incredibly subversive thought.

A: A veiling and masking operation is being performed on Ibn 'Arabī. Christians can read Nietzsche despite his attack on Christianity, whereas orthodox Islam attacks anyone who thinks for themselves. There's an ignorance that transforms knowledge into a crime.

H: How is it that man, who used to play with the gods, got the idea of inventing a god to whom he submitted without any possibility of play? As if there wasn't just a need to believe, but a need for a dogma that stifled him.

A: There are several levels or several layers to man. He is a talking animal, as Aristotle said. The talking being overtakes the animal being. Now, monotheism put more stress on the lower layer, namely the animal. Religion sees man first and foremost as an animal. An animal is instinct centred on itself. And since an animal has no connection with God, God created a prophet as a go-between between himself and this animal, so the latter could rise to the level of the human. In the beginning, Christianity was a revolution on a par with that of Ibn 'Arabī. But the Church instituted Christ. As for Islam, as we've highlighted many times, it copied Judaism.

H: We can't help but observe here that orthodox Islam, which came along after the other two monotheisms, took on only their hateful aspect.

A: The strength of traditionalist Islam was built on man the animal, not man the god. In contrast, Sufism is based on the idea that man is divine. The divine is a call, transcendence, movement and happiness.

H: I really like that word 'call'. For 'Aṭṭār, the *si-morgh* were called to go inside the Simorgh.[18] 'The shadow went into the sun', 'Aṭṭār writes. As for Ḥallāj, he calls the Other like this: 'You who hold everything where. Where are You?'

A: That's quite beautiful, since existing in the sun is an elevated existence. You burn out for a more luminous life.

H: Thanks for that clarification, which I understand as this: it's not about the extermination of the human being, or his annihilation; it's about his effacement. An effacement that gives you more life.

A: In fact, it's about the effacement of all that's animal. Monotheism is linked to power and is thereby a descent towards animality. And so it goes hand in hand with control. That's the reason why monotheism is, in its very essence, political.

H: I remember what you said when we were talking about religion: 'Myth is a question. Religion is an answer.' We might also imagine that mysticism joins myth in that it sparks a questioning that remains open, that is never closed by a single, absolute answer. Ḥallāj's question is a good example.

A: The problem with religion is that it only provides religious answers. Which are exclusive, absolute and final. And that means the cancellation of all enquiry and therefore of all thought. Monotheism is a well, or a tunnel, since it has constructed a small, closed world, like a box, to shut the human being away in. The latter finds himself deprived of his freedom to choose his own path or paths.

H: As opposed to the binary logic that divides individuals into Muslims and infidels, mysticism opts for a path that's more individual, more singular, since each person knows his Lord according to his disposition, according to his inner work and his desire. There's no generalization. How did mysticism arise in Islam in a context dominated by dogma? How was Ibn al-Fāriḍ able to write his great Tā'iya? How was Rūmī able to speak of the divine by giving it the features of his beloved? How could such a subversive and transgressive system of thought see the light of day?

A: As we've already said, Islam began as conquests, confiscations of other people's property, assassinations ... The spiritual element was a revolt against the animal element. Sufism is a form of liberation from that animality. The Sufis opened up questions about the living continuity of the world and the things of this world. As opposed to the split between believers and infidels, they advocated incarnation and thus union. Man becomes the Absolute. And the heart that welcomes the divine is recreated every instant.

H: Ibn 'Arabī said: 'The mystic is a man of his time' for 'God never shows himself to the same person twice' in the sense of a singular, individual moment in time that's forever new, in manifestations that are forever new, never fixed, always in motion, ceaseless.

A: The Absolute remains unknown. When a human being speaks about God, he's not speaking about his essence, but about his manifestation. God appears to every individual in a different, singular way. Man – who can't know the Absolute – knows this manifestation in different existential forms. You can clearly see the difference with the Islam of the *fuqahā'*. All of what we call Muslim civilization, as I've said, was created by non-Muslims: poetry, philosophy, Sufism ... Poets, philosophers and Sufis were badly treated by the political and religious power.

H: One of the great names in the history of Islam is Saladin. He became extremely famous because he was the Saladin of the Crusades, but few people know that he assassinated Suhrawardī, the master of *'ishrāq*.[19] A great loss.

A: Saladin burned down the Fatimid libraries. Yet again, orthodox Islam is against spirituality, just as it showed it was against creativity and innovation.

H: Ḥallāj's assassination and crucifixion – which led Massignon to say he was the Muslim Christ – and the virulent reaction of the *fuqahā'* of Aleppo to Ibn 'Arabī speak volumes about the incompatibility of mystical thought and dogmatic religious thought. Rūmī – who speaks of God as a true Narcissus – said: 'For Sufism to flourish, we would have to close the *madrasah*.'[20]

A: Because he was Persian, he was more radical. Arab-language thinkers and mystics risked being assassinated. As Khayyām said: 'If you punish every sin, what is the difference between us, O Lord?'

H: Al-Nifarī was born in Mesopotamia. Rābi'a lived in Basra (Iraq). Ḥallāj lived in Baghdad. Ibn 'Arabī passed away in Damascus. When you think what total chaos Mesopotamia has become …

A: Sufi thought constitutes another relationship between the Orient and the West, one based on the otherness that is central to the self. In Western monotheist culture, the Orient and the West are two different geographical, political and military entities. But, in Sufi thought, they are two human entities whereby the West cannot be without the Orient and the other way round. In a world beyond politics, economics and geography.

8

The West of the Enlightenment: What Does It Have to Do with the Orient?

H: We can't work on Islam without reflecting on our relationship with the West.

A: All those notions need to be revisited. What is the West? Is the West of the tenth century the same as the West of the twenty-first century? There are several Wests within the West.

H: In that case, we could say the same thing about the Orient.

A: Of course. Those two notions – East, West – need to be reconsidered. Is the West just military and material while the East is spiritual, as naive simplification would have it? Things are much more complex. Geography is no longer defined by terrestrial borders. It's cultural from now on: Shanghai, for instance, can in some respects be more Western than New York.

H: When I saw Greece for the first time, I thought it was the most Oriental of the Western countries.

A: We also need to look at how the East reached the West. The East has done a lot of travelling. You're right, in that regard, Greece is Oriental, not Western. Is the Orient an endless journey? Or is it horizontal while the West is all enquiry and research?

H: The Phoenicians were renowned travellers, but not the Egyptians.

A: Even if they didn't travel, the Egyptians were all about straight lines. We need to analyse everything all over again.

H: Within the scope of this particular project, we can't revisit all these notions, we're merely raising the issue of the complexity of the relations between these two worlds known as the East and the West. The question that won't go away is this: the West has given us the tools to understand our heritage, yet it fights us at the same time.

A: We need to look at today's world and reflect on the link between Islam and the Western world in the light of current conditions. Today, we have a duty not only to analyse the Text and the Islamic corpus, but to analyse Islam within the context of what's happening in Europe and the United States. We need to look at the world as a whole and revisit the issue of Islam within that framework.

H: Let's start, then, with the question that Arabs never stop asking: how can it be that the West of the Enlightenment, of the Industrial Revolution, of the French Revolution and of secularism, today protects Salafism and totalitarian political regimes?

A: The relationship between the West and Islam goes back a fair way. We need to remember first and foremost that Arab Islam rejected the West, from a religious point of view, and rejected its culture. But, on the other hand, it yielded to the West to the point where it became the West's slave as far as politics and economics went. And that's worth looking at in a separate study and analysis. Why does the Arab world put itself through this internal contradiction? It takes what the West produces in terms of technology and rejects the intellect that produces it, thereby fulfilling, perhaps unwittingly, the West's desire: for it to remain in a state of subservience and extreme colonial dependence. The economic and political hegemony of the West is equalled only by the servitude of the Arab world in relation to the West. The balance of power is anything but balanced. Historically, the Orient of the Phoenicians and the Mesopotamians inspired the Greeks who built Western civilization. Well, the West's reaction to the Orient didn't do justice to the Orient's superb generosity.

H: So, the Orient was more into culture, inspiring the West with its alphabet, its science and its mythology, while the West was more at home with economics than with civilization or culture.

A: The West now exploits Islam in order to protect its economic interests, while forgetting all about its most fundamental values, namely human rights, human dignity, freedom of expression, the importance of the other …

H: I recall that it was because of those values that we came to France, or to the West.

A: Well, all those values are now scorned.

H: I'd say: especially when it's a case of applying them in other people's countries …

A: Israel, for example, is a Western country in the sense that the founders were originally from the West. But the

Israeli state exercises a cruelty over the Palestinian people that's reminiscent of the policy of the Whites in relation to the American Indians.

H: In Israel, there's a division between those who came from the East, who were looked down on, and those who came from the West and are more highly regarded.

A: The British poet Kipling said: East is East and West is West, and never the twain shall meet.

H: Was he talking about a clash of civilizations?

A: A clash is already a meeting. Well, the West's relationship with the East has often been based on profit, hegemony and enslavement. But today we can't help but observe the meeting between the East, the Orient – in its Salafist guise – and the West in its American-European version.

H: That's another way of saying that the West only actually deals with the political and institutional Orient that has managed to resist the ideas of the Enlightenment and progress. It prefers it to the Orient of nations that aspire to freedom, democracy and progress.

A: The political West not only deals with dictatorships, but has also eradicated the ideas of the left, especially the enlightened and creative left. In Arab and/or Muslim countries, America has supported Islam in order to fight communism. We could say that the meeting between this political West and the Arab and Muslim Orient is a meeting between decadence and collapse. The West has abandoned its values. It has stood by and watched the extermination of Palestinians without reacting …

H: And without being outraged over the use of arms sold to Saudi Arabia, which uses them to wipe out the Yemen.

A: We're back to the idea according to which the antihuman is what defines the meaning of being human.

H: Lafarge is an example, among others. The French government provided the Islamists with arms in Syria in 2012. It played a part in the chaos that now reigns in Libya …

A: If the truth be known, Islam is useful to Europe and to the United States. It has allowed the West to further develop the tools and methods of colonization. Stage left, the West destabilized Iraq, Syria and Libya, turning them to rubble and ruins. Stage right, we also have to criticize intellectual output in the West, namely the basis of its cultural practice. Take Sartre and Camus, for example …

H: The whole world praised Camus's style. A great many studies have been done on *L'Etranger* (*The Outsider/The Stranger*). Roland Barthes hailed it as a 'stellar novel'. But I still remember that when Malik Oussekine died as a result of police violence after a student demonstration against the Devaquet university reform project in 1986, Jean-Marie Le Pen attacked Malik by saying his sister was 'a prostitute'. That's exactly the reasoning of Meursault's lawyer in Camus's *L'Etranger*. Which is why I pay homage to Kamel Daoud because, before he came along [with his own novel *Meursault, contre-enquête* – *The Meursault Investigation* – in 2013], no one had deconstructed that investigation, which was in fact a show of scorn for the Arab. The man isn't even named [in Camus's novel].

A: Camus translated a mindset that's expressed openly by the extreme right, as a matter of fact. We need seriously to reflect on the way Western identity meshes with Oriental identity.

H: Le Pen said: 'I say out loud what people are quietly thinking to themselves.'

A: Then he was expressing a truth silenced by politics and ideologies. We don't want readers to think we're defending the politics of Islam. We're the first to attack it. That said, I'd like the general hypocrisy to be exposed.

H: Mouloud Feraoun wrote to Camus: 'I understand. Do you understand me?' The question is poignant since it shows the gap between a child of Algeria pained at seeing another who was also born in Algeria but who thought of Oran as nothing more than 'an ordinary French post', in Feraoun's words.

A: Camus had a very ambivalent relationship with Algeria. That's a well-known fact.

H: Speaking of Camus, Edward Said later referred to his 'colonial subconscious', and Kateb Yacine went on to say: 'I prefer a writer like Faulkner, who is sometimes racist but has a Black as one of his heroes, to someone like Camus, who advertises his anticolonial views while Algerians are missing in his work and Algeria, for him, means Tipaza – a landscape.' Obviously, the views of Arab intellectuals and French intellectuals differ. Barthes's later critical piece was concerned with the realism of *La Peste* (*The Plague*) and not the complete absence of Algerians in a novel where the events take place in Oran. It's hurtful to those intellectuals who remember Renan wrote: 'All that the Semitic Orient, all that the Middle Ages have had by way of philosophy, properly so called, they owe to Greece. If it were a matter of choosing a philosophical authority from the past, Greece alone would have the right to teach us lessons; not the Greece of Egypt and Syria, altered by the mixture of barbarian elements, but the original and true Greece, in its pure and classical expression.'

A: Renan saw Semites as barbarians.

H: We find the term 'barbarian' cropping up again under Claudel's pen, completely ignoring all that Arabs have contributed. This is what he writes to Louis Massignon, asking him if there's some truth in what Renan thought about Semites:[1] 'When will you leave that godforsaken place Egypt? I know all about these long solitary posts in the middle of an infuriating country, with nothing that appeals to the imagination except what's diabolical, with no friendly intellectuals … Poor boy! … You live alone in the midst of all those heathens.'[2]

A: And Sartre, for instance, never took the rights of the Palestinian people into consideration. And Levinas never mentioned the Palestinian people, either.

H: It gets very complicated. Today, there are very few things written about the sufferings of the Palestinians, the dismantling of Syria and Iraq, the strikes raining down on Yemen, the chaos in Libya … Arab protesters haven't taken to the streets, either, when faced with images of trucks filled with Yazidi Kurd women. What are we to make of this stance of not being there? Either the extreme violence we see on a daily basis saps all thought, or the people who once fought for a better future, precisely those who formed the left, were exterminated.

A: The West was on the side of IS. It took part in the destruction of Arab countries. It didn't really fight the despots but worked towards the devastation of their countries. Western rulers did indeed eliminate tyrants like Saddam and Gaddafi. Not to set up a democracy, but to stop them from naming out loud the sources that were financing electoral campaigns like the one in Libya. Gaddafi was close to Berlusconi.

H: I'll take this opportunity to remind everyone of Fascist Italy's extreme barbarity in Libya.

A: Today there's a Franco-Italian alliance against Libya's awakening and its aspiration to rise from the rubble. We won't go into the details, though, because we're not political scientists. Let's just remind people that we're involved in a two-pronged attack, since we're in the middle.

H: That's true. Our position is far from comfortable. But it's the same for all intellectuals caught between the regimes of their native countries and the West of the Enlightenment and of hegemony. Today, Kamel Daoud, the man who wrote that counter-investigation, finds himself assailed for taking a stand against Islam. Happily, we still have the support of French people who remain critical of what Elisabeth Badinter calls the position of 'servitude' in relation to Salafist Islam.

A: I'll spell my idea out more clearly: It's the Western antihuman that defines what is human. How does this translate in the East–West relationship? First, globalization, or internationalization, has turned the world into a military barracks and a market for trade and profit yield at the expense of culture. And in this era of globalization, the Arabs have neither industry, nor technology, nor any serious science education.

H: On the subject of globalization, Alain Touraine speaks of fragmentation within societies, rather than conflict, and of an ever-increasing gap between rich and poor.

A: The weak and the poor are seen as burdens within the society and so there's a desire to have done with them.

H: Michel Foucault's remarks about exclusion are still valid. Today, we see this with the refugee and immigrant crisis.

A: Just as if they were the American Indians. We could also talk about a gradual extermination of the Palestinian people.

The Palestinian issue is a living example of the accord and complicity between the Arabs and the American-European West. On top of that, we're seeing the conversion of religion into political capital and into an instrument of hegemony. Religion, having become a powerful weapon in the hands of men in government or greedy for power, has replaced intense spiritual experiences. Religion is used as a bomb or a cannon or a fighter jet, and the so-called culture of discovery and exploration has been turned into an instrument at the service of various regimes. As a result, the human is no longer a goal. Man, too, has become an instrument.

H: Is he an instrument of globalization or of religion and power?

A: The political West has been Islamized, in the bad sense of the term. Take France for example. The spirit of creativity and innovation in the domain of research and thought has declined. We'd have trouble these days finding great minds like Sartre, Deleuze, Foucault …

H: Speaking of this concept of Islamization, the European Court of Human Rights recently legitimized sharia and the Islamic code of 'blasphemy' with regard to Muhammad.[3]

A: We can only deplore this decline on the part of a mind that used to be fired by freedom and creativity but has now been captured by the politico-ideological and the prevailing power. It's turned into a bureaucratic mind like the Arab Muslim mind. Islam died as a spiritual experience in Medina, and now Christianity has also died in Europe. Today's Islam is the kind peddled in Medina. So, the Islam that should have died is the only brand that now prevails. The West is also suffering. The Christianity of revolt, of love, of openness to others and fraternity has been defeated. We could even say that, on this score, Christ has died in Europe. The same way that Mecca has died among Muslims.

H: You're saying that in both worlds (Oriental and Western), spirituality has given up the ghost.

A: Because money has become not only king of the world, but also the world's god.

H: You were talking about the European West and the American West. In his latest book, Régis Debray points to the Americanization of the West. Where is the resistance of intellectuals in the land of Diderot and Voltaire?

A: The United States operates as if it were the world's educator. It can punish any country that disagrees with its positions. This is the triumph of the material, economic-financial aspect.

H: People talk about the world's police.

A: It acts not only as the police, but also as the king of the world. The world is an American property. People operate according to the value of the dollar. The United States would wage war on anyone who ventured to set up a currency independent of the dollar. In actual fact, where is man? Where is culture? Where are human values?

H: Money madness isn't a recent thing. You only have to read Zola's *Money*. And obscurantism has endured through the centuries. We have the examples of Galileo, Copernicus, Ḥallāj, Averroès and many others … Yet man has always shown a capacity for resistance.

A: In the past, rebels were killed and freedom fighters eliminated. Today, the system buys off intellectuals by offering them careers. It's become more perverse. The system allows them to speak, but within a narrowly circumscribed space. On top of that, we note that the political scene has been emptied of leaders who embody resistance and respect for thought and creativity.

H: In a recent issue of *Le Magazine littéraire* dedicated to Michel Foucault, we see a beautiful photo of Sartre and Foucault together. The two philosophers didn't share the same views, but they stood side by side in the Goutte d'or [area of Paris] in support of migrants.

A: The example you give of Sartre and Foucault speaks volumes. It signifies that, in the democratic tradition, when a writer published an article or a book, his opponents debated with him in a spirit of respect.

H: But we could also talk about the support certain French intellectuals have given to people who are fighting for freedom.

A: Yes, of course. I'm just saying that the intellectual no longer really enjoys freedom of expression today. As soon as what he says calls something into question, he finds himself violently attacked.

H: As if there were a single model of thought. That's borne out in other domains. You're supposed to be on a highway and not branch off. But if we go back to the case of Kamel Daoud, it's clear that the intellectual in Arab or Muslim countries is caught in a sandwich. He's disowned at home, and he's also disowned in a country that nevertheless defends freedom of expression. We could say the same thing about Boualem Sansal.

A: Yes: if you express opinions that run counter to the official position, you find yourself rejected. People don't even deign to have a conversation with you. They may even accuse you or discredit you. What happened to plurality? You get the impression that today there's a monotheism not in heaven but on Earth, and it determines everything.

H: You were saying the Muslims didn't follow God's example when he agreed to debate with Satan instead of exterminating him. But we note here that that isn't just the prerogative of Muslims. The absence of democratic dialogue is starting to prevail in the Western world.

A: It's the triumph of the monotheist intellectual orthodoxy. The moment you break the mould, people exclude you rather than debate with you. I feel as if the world is collapsing.

H: It's the triumph of the economy at the expense of human values. And with the problem between the West and the Orient, the economic stakes are – and this is the thing – more important than the charter of human rights. The political West that advocates secularism in the Western world is the first to rise up against freedom of expression when it comes to Islam. We mentioned the European Court of Human Rights, which advocates the defence of sharia.

A: Seen from the point of view of economic interests, the Arab world is, for the West, a hell of a strategic space and a mine of wealth. We need to reflect on the attitude of Europeans to the refugee crisis. Some countries have refused to host refugees even though they've participated in the destruction of their countries – like France – whereas Germany took them in.

H: Children were separated from their parents. They say that six thousand children disappeared in Germany just in 2015 alone; ten thousand refugee minors throughout Europe. There's talk of organized crime (traffic in human organs, prostitution ...). Which represents a major psychological and anthropological upheaval, a human catastrophe.

A: The West is beginning to practise what we criticize in Islam, namely non-recognition of the value of the human person. In Arab and Muslim countries, all you have to do is pronounce a death sentence against an individual for that individual to be exterminated without a trial, or a verdict. Today, the human condition in the West has gone backwards. In that sense, as I said, the West has been Islamized.

H: It's the triumph of totalitarianism, but human beings have always managed to resist. Writing is a form of resistance. Sansal writes: 'How else, without holy ignorance and the total apathy-inducing possession of people's minds, could those poor folk have been persuaded that before the birth of Abistan there was only the uncreated, unknowable universe of Yölah? It couldn't be simpler: just choose a date and stop time at that moment; people are already dead and foundering in the void, they'll believe anything you tell them, they will applaud their rebirth in 2084.'[4] And also: 'How can you tell your own contemporaries, now, that if they carry on the way they've begun yesterday's tragedies will soon be upon them?'[5]

A: In the name of tolerance, we just step back and leave them to it. Instead of thinking in terms of equality, the West is now preaching tolerance. Tolerance implies a feeling of superiority. 'I am tolerant towards you' means 'I am superior to you'. Man needs equality more than tolerance. Sansal is right: yesterday's tragedies can repeat themselves. Especially as freedom of expression is increasingly under attack and human beings find themselves encircled by and within a draconian system. Happily, they continue to resist and the world hasn't been drained of all resistance. There have always been people who said no. Happily

– otherwise, human beings would all turn into instruments and machines. There would be no more creativity or inventiveness. But the situation today is clearly more difficult, more complex, since the world is doing without mankind more and more. The world is becoming more mechanical, more 'machinized'.

H: *Quand on refuse on dit non* (*When we refuse we say no*).[6] There is certainly a crisis, but man has always resisted. Even in the darkest science fiction novels, man shows a capacity for resistance – *2084*, which extends the thinking behind George Orwell's *1984*, can be read as a call to resistance.

A: Indeed. And our work is a form of resistance. As in the book by Ibn Ṭufayl, *Ḥayy ibn Yaqẓān*,[7] the world will go on living as long as there are human beings. But what worries me today is the hegemony of intellectual orthodoxy, reductionism and simplification. Individuality and differences are erased in favour of terms with no real meaning.

H: Foucault denounced this way of lumping all the undesirables together willy-nilly. When we say Jews, Muslims ... when we talk in terms of identity, we're in that state of non-distinction and confusion.

A: Michel Foucault's work is a form of resistance. And our work is a form of resistance. Such is life. Sometimes, it's the dark side that wins, sometimes, it's the light!

H: The eternal duel of Eros and Thanatos. Todorov wrote a book called *Insoumis* (*Unbowed*). He cites people who fought against Nazism, Stalinism and obscurantism, but no Arab name appears. Is that because Westerners don't know the Arab corpus or because ethnocentrism has banished it from its thinking?

A: The history of the Arab world is full of unbowed rebels who paid with their lives: poets, mystics, philosophers, men of science … Arab and Muslim societies have had extremely brilliant men who were forced to disguise their learning or their ideas. The philosophers, for instance, took up Greek thought to be able to philosophize. The list is extremely long. There have always been rebels opposed to religious and political power.

H: So, these victims of politico-religious power are today victims of ethnocentrism.

A: You won't find in all of Europe a poet as rebellious as al-Mutanabbī, for example. He was against power and against the whole cultural heritage.

H: *Lā nabiyya baʿdī wa ʿanā lā.*[8] What force, what blasphemy, and what a magnificent play on language! Poetry ignores taboos.

A: 'Whoever is ignorant of his true worth / Sees it reflected in the other's eyes.'[9]

H: His language was unique. And the way you weave him into a face-to-face with Imru' al-Qais is sublime. Yet, only a person who knows that corpus can grasp the power and beauty of this poetic face-to-face. Well, al-Mutanabbī is not part of the Western intellectual fabric, any more than Imru' al-Qais is. We find ourselves confronted by a world that defends a religion in the name of Arab greatness yet continues to ignore what makes for that greatness. I might add that we continue to be ignored unless we align ourselves with Western politics. Consequently, I can only exist if I renounce my revolt, my corpus, my plurality. It's all very complex. For we no longer belong *stricto senso* to Arab culture: moving to the West has changed us and yet, this

West that gives me the tools to think with only accepts me if I align myself with its own thought. The West therefore remains our place of shelter and our source of suffering. The Arab creator belongs to a social and intellectual fabric that is no longer what it was in the beginning, and he doesn't really count for Westerners. He's in a space in-between.

A: We could sum up the American-European attitude regarding an Arab creator by saying that it regards him first as an Arab, and only then as a creator. That attitude is racist. There is racism and contempt for the humanity of the human being. But we can also say that any human being who despises the other actually despises himself.

Epilogue: Leaving the Cave!

What we didn't want to do in *Violence and Islam* is criticize religion as a relationship between the individual and his god. We defend the right to belief – on condition that it doesn't encroach upon the freedom of others. But if man has the right to believe, he also has the right not to believe. And in civil society, this right deserves to be respected and must be respected.

We criticize the ideology of politico-religious hegemony that is turning the world into a system closed in on itself in contempt for the freedoms of individuals, and we continue to fight for the emergence – in the Arab and Muslim world – of a civil, secular society in which the individual is free to think, to express himself and to live in respect and dignity.

Hence our insistence in these two volumes of *Violence and Islam* on the obligation for Muslims of turning 'legend history into work history'. This requires a courageous and radical confrontation with a whole raft of issues that we can't sum up in their entirety; we can't even deal with the majority of them, but we can raise three.

First, history has shown that a society that has religion as its basis and foundation is, by definition, an unjust society, even if it opts for tolerance. This latter necessarily implies the superiority of one section of the society in relation to another section, seen as weaker, less enlightened, more vulnerable, less advanced … As well as this, tolerance risks obscuring injustice and exclusion. Man needs equality more than tolerance.

Second, religion was invented for man. This explains the plurality of religious beliefs. But Muslims live in societies that, through their politico-legal and social institutions, practise beliefs and rites that work the other way round (man is created for religion). This is why we pause on this verse, 'I have not created jinn and mankind except to serve Me',[1] which contradicts this other verse: 'The truth is from your Lord; so let whosoever will believe, and let whosoever will disbelieve.'[2] Which verse are we supposed to follow? And which verse abrogates the other?

We've quoted several verses that are characterized by their extreme cruelty in relation to man, a cruelty liable to produce terror, dread and psychological anaesthesia – verses such as:

> Then the unbelievers shall be driven in companies into Gehenna
> till, when they have come thither, then its gates will be opened …
> It shall be said: 'Enter the gates of Gehenna, to dwell therein
> Forever.' How evil is the lodging of those that are proud![3]

And

> … As for the unbelievers,
> for them garments of fire shall be cut,
> and there shall be poured over their heads
> boiling water
> whereby whatsoever is in their bellies

> and their skins shall be melted; for them await
> hooked iron rods;
> as often as they desire in their anguish
> to come forth from it, they shall be restored
> into it, and: 'Taste the chastisement
> of the burning!'[4]

Building power on religion is in itself an act of violence and a waste of civilizational and human resources. The prohibition on thinking has kept Muslims, broadly speaking, in a mental state of submission or voluntary servitude (to borrow La Boétie's expression). And those who have rebelled against the political and religious dictatorship (saying: if man is created in the image of God and perpetrates injustice, tyranny and despotism, what sense do we give to the divinity?) have paid with their lives. Result: the more the world advances, the more Muslims regress.

Third, the ways of thinking that have fostered inventiveness, creativity and progress in the Arab and Muslim world, over fifteen centuries, did not derive from the Text or the *fiqh*,[5] even if they dressed themselves up in Islamic garb. As for their essence, that is made of a different clay. Sufism really rocked the religious structure to the core. It managed to move the Muslim world from a poor system that was closed in on itself to a different system, one open to human experience, the expanses and broad vistas of reflection and thinking around forbidden themes: divinity, humanity, an identity fashioned by otherness, language, the spirit of the word, the image … Subversiveness gave this corpus, and also philosophy and poetry, endless effulgence.

And so, if we venture this question: what is Muslim culture, strictly speaking? The answer is: It's not poetry, or philosophy, or mysticism, or the art of photography, it's not dance, or music or singing. What's left? The *fiqh* and the *shar*ʿ.

Where Descartes says, 'I think, therefore I am', in light of the above, the Muslim says: 'I'm a Muslim, I observe the precepts of Islam, I imitate the Prophet and his first companions. Therefore, I am.' 'Islamically' speaking, this comes down to saying: 'Invent nothing, follow and imitate.'

It's that core (of Islamic culture) on which identity in Islam rests that we've been trying to deconstruct. Identity becomes an imitation. And indeed, a call for an all-out imitation that prevents any individual autonomy, prevents the Muslim from adapting to changes in society, from reflecting on the world's upheavals, and from taking part in the march of time. He's like a child who refuses to grow up. Even when it comes to sexuality, he's supposed to imitate the Prophet. Doubt is a blasphemy, and dissidence is prohibited and punishable by the death penalty.

If every religion has its share of violence and cruelty, Islam is confronted with the problem of how its history was written and passed on. What is it a matter of remembering? Whose memory is it? These questions come up against not only the taboo on thinking about the Text, but also against 'egology', that is, the sacredness of the first transmitters, the first caliphs and the hagiographers. Their memory becomes the sacred History. You can't refute, or judge. This has had a negative effect on the construction of a genuine science of history. Well, what was begun by Ibn Khaldūn and Averroès – writing that the world could not be explained by religion alone – and by Rāwandī and many other intellectuals, must be continued and extended today.

But, instead of pursuing work begun by individuals who fought for the spread of thought, the *fuqahā'*[6] are advocating a return to an unsullied beginning and espousing the cause of identity, forgetting (or ignoring) the fact that identity – and the notion of a beginning – are constructions that are always on the move, never fixed. In actual fact, the *fuqahā'* – inviting Muslims to rediscover a phantasmatically ideal past – are in danger of shutting them away like cave people,[7] in a timelessness outside the march of human history, with no way of being able to construct a present or a future for themselves and for their descendants.

Muslims need to reread their Text in light not only of abrogation, of the contradictions between different verses, of anachronism … but bearing in mind the convulsions that have occurred in civilization: secularism, the Charter of Human Rights. They must reflect on and reconsider verses that make the assassination of 'unbelievers' legal, or that allow women to be mistreated or deprived of equal rights. The language itself must evolve, since it remains stuck in a primitive time and in an archaic vision of society. To give an example, the word virgin (*'adhrā*) is to this day only used in the feminine, as if boys were born men, as if there was no historic journey for them to take; *muṭallaqa* (a repudiated wife) is the legal term designating a divorced woman. Well, the grammatical schema indicates that she undergoes the action even if she's the one instituting it. This is to say nothing about words taken straight from some bestiary, words such as unattached she-camels or ewes, grazing at will.

In the light of today's culture, and archaeological discoveries, we can't just keep on saying that the earlier pre-Islamic period was a time of *jāhiliyya*[8] and that we are 'the best nation'. 'The psyche must resolve to represent the real state of the outside world and to envisage bringing real change to it. What is represented is no longer what is agreeable, but what is real, despite the displeasure this may entail.'[9]

One example among thousands of others: 'Two Australian mathematicians think the Plimpton 322 tablet, engraved three thousand seven hundred years ago in cuneiform script, is in fact a trigonometric tablet of a new kind, the most precise ever formulated!' we read today. How, in the age of information technology, hi-tech and progress on all levels and in all domains, can we go on reciting verses on the *jāhiliyya* as absolute truth?

We are fighting for a form of secularism, specifically for the separation of the religious sphere from the political, legal and social domains. In this day and age, we can no longer say that the Text has answered all questions, that it is universal and timelessly right for the whole Earth. 'Our age *knows better* ... What was formerly merely sickly now becomes indecent.'[10]

Glossary

'aḍḍād	Words with opposite meanings
'adhāb	Torture
'adhrā	Virgin
al-'alaq	'The blood clot': Qur'an 96:1.
al-baṭsh	Tyranny, extermination
Al-Burāq	Winged horse with the face of a woman which carried Muhammad to seventh heaven
al-ḥanīfiyya	In pre-Islamic South Arabia, the word referred to the religion preached by Maslama al-Ḥanafī
al-hudā	The right path
al-isrā'	Muhammad's nocturnal journey from Mecca to Jerusalem in a single night
al-madīna al-faḍīla	The virtuous city, as imagined by Al-Fārabī (872–950), founder of political philosophy in the medieval Arab and Muslim world
al-mi'rāj	Muhammad's ascent to seventh heaven, the same night as *al-isrā'*
Al-muddaththir	'The Shrouded': Qur'an 74:1–56

Al-Wāhid	God the One
amāna	Faithfulness
'an'ana	Oral series naming the people who handed down a *hadīth* or commentary on a Qur'anic verse
An-Nûr	The Light, the name of God
Anṣâr	Includes the people of Medina who welcomed and supported Muhammad and the people of Mecca who converted to Islam
Asharite school	A theological school of Islam founded by Abū l'Hasan al-Ash'arī (260–324 Hijra Era)
aṣṣirâṭ	The straight path
attaba'iyya	Blind, unquestioning conformity, a rule that Muslims must apply in order to follow Muhammad as a role model who submitted to God's will, and the Prophet's companions, seen as perfect or accomplished men
Banū Hāshim	Muhammad's family, the Hashemites
Batinites	Followers of an esoteric school of thought embraced by the Ismailis and the Qarmatians
bilā kayf	'Without asking how', used in theology by the Asharites to solve the issue of God's anthropomorphism
dīn wa dunyā	Religion and life
diya	Blood money
Fadak	Land promised by Muhammad to his daughter Fatima as a bequest
farj	Sex
fiqh	Islamic law

fuqahā'	Theolgians specializing in Islamic law
ghazawāt	Conquests
ḥadīth	Saying of Muhammad
ḥadīth qudsī	God speaking through the mouth of Muhammad
hafazat al-Qur'an	Apprentices of the Qur'an who learn it by heart
Hājar	(Agar in the Old Testament): the wife of Abraham and mother of Ishmael
ḥajjat al-wadā'	Muhammad's farewell pilgrimage
ḥākim	A ruler or person exercising some form of political power
ḥanīf	Original, pure; later used in reference to Islam, understood as the pure religion (*ḥanīfiyya*)
houris	Voluptuous women peopling paradise
huyām	Passionate love
Iblīs	Satan
Imam	Muslim dignitary who directs common prayer
'ishrāq	Illumination
jāhiliyya	Time of ignorance, qualifying the pre-Islamic period marked by paganism
jaḥīm	Gehenna/hell
jamā'a	Community
janna	Paradise
jāriya	Female slave, who was both a musician and a dancer
jinn	Spirit or genie
Ka'ba	The Black Rock, a place of pilgrimage in Mecca
kabbarū	Glorifying God by using

	the expression 'Allah 'akbar' ('God is the greatest')
khanādiq	Trenches (plural of *khandaq*)
khayāl	Imagination
muhājir	Emigrant from Mecca
muntaqim	Avenger
muṭallaqa	A wife whose husband has formally repudiated her
Mu'tazilite school	Formed in Basra as early as the first half of the second century Hijra Era, it became a leading school of speculative theology
nafsahā	Soul
nāqil	Someone who transmits the Qur'an
naskh	Abrogation
Qarmatians	A dissident political sect of the Fatimid dynasty, fourth century Hijra Era
Quraysh, Qurayshites	The Meccan tribe to which Muhammad's family belonged
rāshidūn	The Sages, referring to the first four caliphs: Abū Bakr, Umar ibn al-Khattāb, 'Uthmān ibn 'Affan and 'Alī ibn Abī Tālib
ridda	Apostasy
saby	Taking captives and prisoners of war
ṣadīd	Pus
Ṣaḥīḥ Muslim	One of the main collections of *hadīth* in Sunni Islam
ṣaqar	Boiling water
Saqīfa (Banī Sā'ida)	Place where the oath of allegiance to Abū Bakr, the first caliph after Muhammad's death, was sworn
Shafi'ite school	School of Islamic law founded by Muslim lawyer and scholar

	Abū Abdullah Muhammad ibn Idris al- Shaf'i (767–820)
Shām	Present-day Syria
sharḥ	Opening
shar'	Islamic law
sharia	Canons of Islamic law that are applied to religious, political, social and private life
siḥr	Magic
sunna	Precepts and practices of Muhammad
tābi	An uncritical follower (see *attaba'iyya*)
taqwīl	Making someone say what you want them to say
ṭayr abābīl	In the imaginary Muslim realm, these are birds that defended the Ka'ba before the advent of Islam
tijāra	Commerce, trade
Umayyads	Dynasty of caliphs founded in Damascus by Mu'āwiya ibn 'Abī Sufyān (602–680)
'ummī	Illiterate person
'Uthmān's Qur'an	Version of the Qur'an retained by Muhammad's son-in-law, who became the third caliph. It is the commonly accepted version of the Text
Wahhabism	Political and religious sect founded in Saudi Arabia by Muhammad ben Abdelwahhab in the thirteenth century and preaching a rigorist, puritanical brand of Islam
Wasq	Unit of measure
wathanī	Pagan
wi'ā	Receptacle

wizr	Burden
Zanj	Bantu-speaking slaves; the Zanj Rebellion took place in 255 Hijra Era in the reign of the Abbasids

Notes

Chapter 1 God, 'The Messenger of Muhammad'?

1 Adonis, *Violence and Islam: Conversations with Houria Abdelouahed*, Oxford, Polity, 2016.

2 Words of Muhammad. Unless otherwise indicated, translations from the Arabic are by Houria Abdelouahed [with translations from the French by the translator except where other published English translations exist].

3 'We believe in God, and in that which has been sent down on us and sent down on Abraham, Ishmael, Isaac and Jacob, and the Tribes, and that which was given to Moses and Jesus and the Prophets, of their Lord; we make no division between any of them, and to Him we surrender': (Qur'an 2:136). [The English translation cited in this book is the famous one done by classicist Arthur J. Arberry for Oxford World's Classics in 1964. Titled *The Koran*, it has been reissued many times since. Arberry tends to arrange verses eccentrically in bunches, but the basis is fundamentally the same. There are more modern translations available, including one published in 2008 in the Oxford World's Classics series by Abdel Haleem. Translator's note.]

4 'Some of the Jews pervert words from their meanings …

twisting with their tongues and traducing religion': Qur'an 4:46.

5 Qur'an 5:13.

6 Qur'an 4:157.

7 The precepts and daily practices of Muhammad.

8 Qur'an 3:19.

9 *Raḍītulakum al-'islām dīnan.* This phrase can be translated several ways: 'I chose Islam as religion for you'; 'I opted for Islam as a religion for you'; 'I blessed Islam as a religion for you.'

10 Qur'an: 3:110.

11 'Some of the Jews pervert words from their meanings': Qur'an 4:46.

12 Qur'an 3:67: 'Abraham in truth was not a Jew, neither a Christian; but he was a Muslim and one pure of faith.'

13 Qur'an: 3:19.

14 We prefer to talk of the *shar'* to emphasize its Muslim specificity, rather than of the law, meaning the whole set of rules and precepts of Islam.

15 See note 7.

16 Community.

17 Abū Abdallah Muhammad ibn Idris al-Shafi'i was born in Palestine in 767, and died in Egypt in 820. He was a lawyer and Muslim scholar and founder of the school of Shafi'ite *fiqh* (Muslim law).

18 Original, pure. See the Qur'an 2:135; 3:67, 395; 4:125; 6:79, 161; 10:105; 16:120, 123; 30:30; 22:31; 98:5.

19 We pay tribute here to Muhammad Mahmūd's courage and his meticulous work, *Nubuwat Mohammad. At-tarīkh wa as-sina'a* (*The Prophecy of Mohammed. History and Construction*), Centre for Critical Research on Religion, London, 2013.

20 The tribe to which Muhammad belonged.

21 Cited in Mahmūd, *Nubuwat Mohammad*, p. 89.

22 The sum of so-called genuine precepts of Muhammad's.

23 Cf. Mahmūd, *Nubuwat Mohammad*, p. 89, note 3.

24 Abū 'Uthmān 'Amru ibn Bahr was a Mu'tazilite writer and

encyclopédiste; he was born in Bassora (Iraq) in 776 and died in 867.

25 'Did we not expand thy breast for thee and lift from thee thy burden, the burden that weighed down thy back? Did we not exalt thy fame?': Qur'an 94:1–4.

26 Ibn Muzāḥim al-Hilālī was a commentator on the Qur'an. He died in Balkh (Persia) in the year 102 or 105 or 106 Hijra.

27 Qutāda ibn Da'āma al-Sadūsī, who died in 736, was a commentator and reciter of *ḥadīths*.

28 Cf. Mahmūd, *Nubuwat Mohammad*, p. 91.

29 Qur'an 93:7.

30 Cf. note 18.

31 Ma'rūf al-Ruṣāfī (1875–1945) was an Iraqi poet.

32 'Hast thou not seen how thy Lord did with the Men of the Elephant? Did he not make their guile to go astray? And he loosed upon them birds in flights, hurling against them stones of baked clay and He made them like green blades devoured': Qur'an 105:1–5.

33 Two rival tribes in South Arabia that settled in Yathrib (which became Medina) probably around AD 300. The Khazraj were to form the future core of the Ansar (Muhammad's followers).

34 Cf. Qur'an 46:29, 72:1.

35 The Book of Daniel, 8:16, 12:7. [The Holy Bible, King James edition. All biblical quotes are from this edition. Translator's note.]

36 In the Gospel of St Luke, Gabriel announces to Zachariah that his wife Elizabeth will have a son (John), and he also announces the birth of Jesus to Mary.

37 Muhammad's family.

38 Ibn Sa'd, *Ṭabaqāt*, I, Maktabat al-Khanjī, Cairo, 2001, p. 162.

39 Qur'an 51:56.

40 Ibn Manẓūr (b.1233), *Lisān al-'Arab*, 9 vols, *Dār al-Ma'ārif*, Cairo, root: *s.l.m.*

41 Qur'an 54:2.

42 Qur'an 51:52.

43 *Taqwīl* is the act of making someone say what you want.

Chapter 2 The *Ghazawāt*: The Violence Involved in the Foundation of Islam

1 Conquests.
2 Ibn Hishām (who died in 213 Hijra Year), *Kitāb al-sīra al-nabawiyya*, Dār al-maʿrifa li-l-ṭabʿa wa al-nashr, Beirut, 1976.
3 Al-Wāqidī (who died in 207 Hijra Year), *Kitāb al-maghāzī*, I, Dār al-kutub al-ʿilmiyya, Beirut, pp. 187–8.
4 The people of Medina who offered a refuge to Muhammad and to the Meccans who had converted to Islam.
5 Muʿāwiya ibn ʾAbī Sufyān, the founder of the Umayyad dynasty whose capital was Damascus. He was born in Mecca in 602 and died in Damascus in 680.
6 A unit of measure.
7 The Battle of Badr took place on 17 Ramaḍān, in the second century Hijra Era (13 March 624).
8 The 7 Shawwāl in 3 Hijra Year, 23 March 625.
9 Ibn Hishām, *Al-sīra*, 2, p. 636.
10 Al-Wāqidī, *Kitāb al-maghāzī*, I, p. 79.
11 Mahmūd, *Nubuwat Muhammad*, p. 164.
12 Qur'an 93: 6–8.
13 Qur'an 3:169.
14 Qur'an 47:12.
15 Qur'an 56: 20–21.
16 Qur'an 55:54.
17 Abrogation.
18 The verse goes on to say: 'that is better for you and purer. Yet if you find not the means, God is all-forgiving, all-compassionate': Qur'an 58:12.
19 Blind conformity.

Chapter 3 Putting the Text to Work

1 Qur'an 94:1.
2 Opening.
3 Muhammad's journey from Mecca to Jerusalem in a single night.
4 Muhammad's ascension or climb up to seventh heaven (the same night as *al-isrā*).

5 Qur'an 17:1.
6 Qur'an 51:52.
7 Muhammad's son-in-law, who became the third caliph.
8 Qur'an 74:1–56.
9 Qur'an 96:1–19.
10 'O believers, take not Jews and Christians as friends': Qur'an 5:51.
11 'Thou wilt surely find the most hostile of men to the believers are the Jews and the idolaters': Qur'an 5:82.
12 'And they are cursed for what they have said': Qur'an 5:64.
13 'Guide us in the straight path, the path of those whom Thou hast blessed, not of those against whom Thou art wrathful, nor of those who are astray': Qur'an 1:6–7.
14 Qur'an 3:67.
15 Epistle to the Romans, 7:14–15.
16 Law.
17 Qur'an 20:113; see also Qur'an 12:2, 13:37, 39:28, 41:3, 42:7, 43:3.
18 Qur'an 93:3.
19 Abrogation.
20 Qur'an 2:106.
21 Abrogation.
22 Qur'an 58:12.
23 Qur'an 3:102.
24 Qur'an 64:16.
25 Qur'an 75:16.
26 Someone who transmits the Qur'an.
27 '… and surely it is a Book Sublime; falsehood comes not to it from before it nor from behind it; a sending down from One All-wise, All-laudable': Qur'an 41:41–2.
28 Cf. Note 25.
29 Qur'an 20:113. See also 'Those are the signs of the Manifest Book. We have sent it down as an Arabic Qur'an; haply you will understand': Qur'an 12:1; and 16:103, 26:195, 12:2, 13:37, 39:28, 41:3, 42:7, 46:12.
30 The straight path.

31 The song is by Sayed Makkawi, an Egyptian singer-songwriter; it was very famous in the 1970s.

32 'And those you fear to be rebellious, admonish; banish them to their couches, and beat them [*iḍrubūhunna*]', says the verse on women: Qur'an 4:34.

33 To hit or beat.

34 'We said, "O fire, be coolness and safety for Abraham!"': Qur'an 21:69.

35 Qur'an 19:35.

36 Muslim theologian, author of the Great Commentary on the Qur'an; he was born in Ray, Persia in 1150, and died in 1210.

37 Fakhr al-Dīn al-Rāzī, *Mafātīh al-Ghayb* [The Keys to the Invisible]. *Histoire des magiciens et de la magie dans le Coran*, Cairo, 1985, p. 47.

38 Genies or spirits.

39 Gehenna (hell), pus (purulence), boiling water, torture.

40 Qur'an 38:57.

41 Tyranny, extermination.

42 '... marry such women as seem good to you, two, three or four': Qur'an 4:3.

43 Her vagina (*ahā* is a possessive suffix meaning 'her', while *farj* means 'vagina'). Qur'an 66:12.

44 Moustapha Safouan, *Pourquoi le monde arabe n'est-il pas libre? Politique de l'écriture et terrorisme religieux*, Paris, Denoël, 2008.

45 Gehenna/hell.

46 Qur'an 4:56.

47 Qur'an 69:24.

48 Qur'an 7:54.

49 In other words, a Muslim must resign himself to not asking the 'how' question.

50 Qur'an 112:3.

51 Adonis, *Le Livre III (Al-Kitāb)*, Paris, Seuil, 2015, translated from Arabic by Houria Abdelouahed.

52 'You are the best nation ever brought forth to men': Qur'an 3:110.

53 Qur'an 8:17.

54 Al-Fārābī was born in Transoxiana in 872, and died in Damascus in 950. He was one of the major figures of medieval philosophy and was nicknamed Magister Secundus, Aristotle being Magister Primus.
55 Abū l-'alā' al-Ma'arrī was a philosopher poet; he was born in southern Aleppo in 979 and died in 1058.
56 Specialists in Islamic law.
57 Islamic law.
58 Without asking how.
59 Born in 752, he was the first great thinker of Mu'tazilite theology.
60 *The Fixed and the Transformative.*

Chapter 4 Saqīfa: Power in a Tizzy

1 An oral sequence that names the people who have passed on a *ḥadīth* or commentary on a Qur'anic verse. According to so-and-so according to so-and-so according to so-and-so … and so on.
2 'Assuredly God knows those who speak truly, and assuredly He knows the liars': Qur'an 29:3.
3 Belonging to the Banū Hāshim, Muhammad's family.
4 Hela Ouardi, *Les Derniers jours de Muhammad*, Paris, Albin Michel, 2016.
5 Illiterate.
6 Qur'an 3:144.
7 Syria.
8 The Truthful One.
9 Sages. This refers to the first four caliphs: Abū Bakr, Umar ibn al-Khaṭṭāb, 'Uthmān ibn 'Affān, Alī ibn Abī Ṭālib.
10 Saqīfa (Banī Sā'ida) is the place where the oath of allegiance to Abū Bakr was sworn after Muhammad's death.
11 Religion and life.
12 '[…] the founding of the Mohammedan religion seems to him to be an abbreviated repetition of the Jewish one, in imitation of which it made its appearance … The inner development of the new religion, however, soon came to a standstill, perhaps because it lacked the profundity

which in the Jewish religion resulted from the murder of its founder': Sigmund Freud, *Moses and Monotheism*, Leonardo Paolo Lovari, 2016.

13 Adonis, *Le Regard d'Orphée*, conversation with Houria Abdelouahed, Paris, Fayard, 2009.

14 Cf. *Violence and Islam*, pp. 6–8.

Chapter 5 The City of God and Entitlement

1 Qur'an 2:256.

2 Qur'an 8:65.

3 Qur'an 51:56.

4 Qur'an 4:48.

5 Specialists in Muslim law (*fiqh*).

6 Apprentices of the Qur'an.

7 Qur'an 5:40.

8 Qur'an 61:10.

9 The taking of captives.

10 Qur'an 61:12.

11 Qur'an 3:19.

12 Qur'an 60:3.

13 Qur'an 3:178.

14 Qur'an 35:8.

15 Qur'an 64:11.

16 Qur'an 3:12.

17 Abrogation.

18 Qur'an 3:197.

19 The Emperor of Persia.

20 A. Saqqāf, *Al-dīn fī shibh al-jazīra al-ʿarabiyya* (Religion in the Arabian Peninsula), Dār al-intishār al-ʿarabī, Beirut, 2004, p. 325.

21 Satan.

22 Including the Ishmaelites and the Qarmatians. They claimed to be seeking the esoteric sense of the Qur'an.

23 Blood money.

24 Friedrich Nietzsche, *Beyond Good and Evil: Prelude to a Philosophy of the Future*, Cambridge, Cambridge University Press, 2002, translated by Judith Norman, p. 55.

Chapter 6 Tillage? Woman, the Most Noble of Words

1 Meister Eckart.
2 Fidelity.
3 Between the Qurayshites and 'Alī's supporters, in 656.
4 A receptacle.
5 Tha'ālibī died in 1038. *Qiṣaṣ al-'anbiyā'* (Stories of the Prophets), Dār al-kutub al-'ilmiyya, 1994.
6 A governor or person exercising a form of political power.
7 A time of ignorance.
8 *Le Diwan de la poésie arabe classique*, Paris, Gallimard, 2008, translated by Houria Abdelouahed, edited and prefaced by Adonis.
9 Ibid., p. 138.
10 Ibid., p. 121.
11 Qur'an 33:33.
12 Qur'an 2:223.
13 Qur'an 4:34.
14 Paradise.
15 Adonis, *Commencement du corps, fin de l'océan* (Start of the body, end of the ocean), Paris, Mercure de France, 2004, translated into French from the Arabic by Vénus Khoury-Ghata.
16 Qur'an 38:53.
17 This quote appears on p. 6 of the original Arab version of *Commencement du corps, fin de l'océan*; it was omitted from the French translation.
18 Wallāda bint al-Mustakfī was a female poet, who was born in Cordoba in 994 and died in 1091.
19 Qur'an 33:37.
20 Passionate love.
21 God willing, in the name of God. The second term is the beginning of the suras.

Chapter 7 'Love's Capital Is Not to Have Any'

1 First Epistle to the Corinthians, 13:1,13.
2 'O believers, whosoever of you turns from his religion, God will assuredly bring a people He loves and who love

Him, humble towards the believers, disdainful towards the unbelievers, men who struggle in the path of God': Qur'an 5:54.

3 Lawyers specializing in Muslim law, doctors of law.

4 Al-Nifarī, *Livre des extases*, Paris, Les Belles Lettres, 2017, translated by Adonis and Donatien Grau.

5 'Sterile any place that does not accept the feminine.'

6 The Muslim imagination, which depicted Al-Buraq ('a winged horse with the face of a woman'), the horse that took Muhammad to seventh heaven in a single night, was in fact inspired by this sculpture from Mesopotamian Antiquity.

7 Qur'an 85:22.

8 An expression used by Ibn 'Arabī. Cf. Michel Chodkiewicz, *Un océan sans rivage*, Paris, Seuil, 1992.

9 Ibn 'Arabī, *The Universal Tree and the Four Birds.*

10 Ibn 'Arabī, *Futūḥāt al-makkiyya* (Illuminations from Mecca) was first published thanks to the emir Abdel-Kader.

11 Imagination.

12 The light.

13 Illuminations from Mecca (cf. Note 10).

14 Akbar is an adjective applied to Ibn 'Arabī, known as Doctor Maximus.

15 The absent or unknown.

16 Interpreter of Desires.

17 'Aṭṭār was a Persian poet and mystic; he died in 1190.

18 'Aṭṭār, *The Conference of the Birds*, New York, Norton, 2017, translated by Sholeh Wolpé. The Simorgh is a fabulous bird that other birds seek and end up finding inside themselves. Si-morgh otherwise means 'thirty birds'.

19 Illumination. Cf. among others, Henry Corbin, *En islam iranien. Aspects spirituels et philosophiques. 2. Sohrawardi et les platoniciens de Perse*, Paris, Gallimard, 'Tel', 1991.

20 Qur'anic schools.

Chapter 8 The West of the Enlightenment: What Does It Have to Do with the Orient?

1 Paul Claudel, Letter of 27 May, 1911.

2 Letter of 10 May 1910.
3 Cf. Jacques Henric's editorial in *Artpress*, January 2019.
4 Boualem Sansal, *2084: The End of the World*, Europa Editions, 2017, translated by Alison Anderson, pp. 229–30.
5 Ibid., p. 231.
6 The title of a novel in French (untranslated) by Ahmadou Kourouma (Paris, Seuil, 2004), who is also the author of *Allah is Not Obliged*, William Heinemann, 2006.
7 *L'Éveillé ou le philosophe autodidacte*, Paris, Libretto No. 561, 2017.
8 '*Lā* (no) prophet after me, and I am *lā* ("no").' ['No prophet after me, and I am none', with a subtext that could be taken to mean 'I am the prophet after Muhammad'.]
9 *Le Diwan de la poésie arabe classique*, p. 208.

Epilogue: Leaving the Cave!

1 Qur'an 51:56.
2 Qur'an 18:29.
3 Qur'an 39:71, 40:76.
4 Qur'an 22:19–22.
5 Islamic law.
6 Specialists in Muslim law.
7 Qur'an 18:1–110.
8 Ignorance.
9 Sigmund Freud, 'Principes au cours des événements psychiques', *Résultats, idées, problèmes, I, 1890–1920*, Paris, PUF, 1984.
10 Friedrich Nietzsche, *The Antichrist*, New York, Knopf, 1920, translated by H. L. Mencken, p. 109.